*Maria Gullberg*

# CROCHET SQUARES

MAGICAL PATTERNS FOR
CLOTHES, ACCESSORIES
& THE HOME

BATSFORD

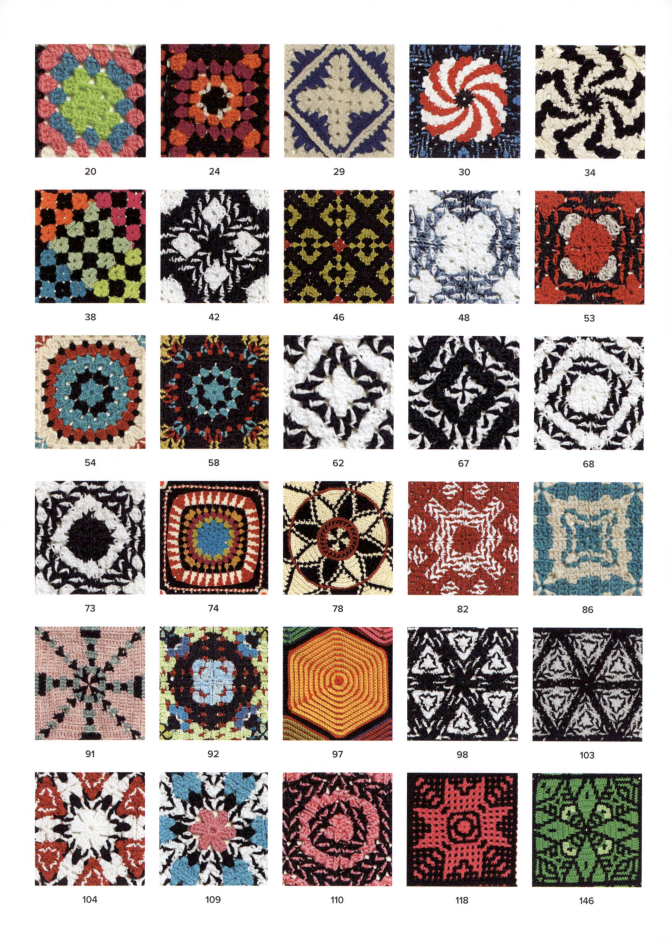

# Contents

- **5** Crochet squares!
- **7** Crochet hooks
- **8** Stitches
- **14** Tips and tricks

## 17 GRANNY SQUARES
- **18** How to read crochet charts
- **19** Key to symbols

| | | | | | | | |
|---|---|---|---|---|---|---|---|
| 21 | *Fighter* | 45 | *Waldemar* | 69 | *Acke* | 93 | *Alina* |
| 25 | *Ulla-Bella* | 49 | *Agda* | 71 | *Zola* | 95 | *Torild* |
| 27 | *Brother Roger* | 51 | *Hilda* | 75 | *Mateo* | 99 | *Fingal* |
| 31 | *Lollipop* | 55 | *Dialogue* | 79 | *Bahia* | 101 | *Trickster* |
| 35 | *Twist* | 59 | *Delight* | 83 | *Svea* | 105 | *Agaton* |
| 39 | *Pillerull* | 63 | *Jambo* | 87 | *Alfhild* | 107 | *Daisy* |
| 43 | *Tora* | 65 | *Aida* | 89 | *Xara* | 111 | *Dainty* |

## 115 MOSAIC CROCHET
- **116** How to read crochet charts
- **117** Key to symbols

| | | | |
|---|---|---|---|
| 119 | *Stella* | 147 | *William Morris* |

- **160** Basic patterns for clothes
- **164** Assembly
- **167** Colours
- **168** Creativity and inspiration

4

# Crochet squares!

This is a book about how to crochet different types of squares and use them for whatever you want! A square is a small crochet project, easy to take with you and very versatile. When you put several squares together and create a repeating pattern, magic happens! Squares can be for beginners and experts alike.

Everything is here, from the classic granny square and its variations, to more advanced mosaic crochet squares. They can be square, but also hexagonal or half squares, and can all be put together to create different patterns.

Squares are often assembled to make a throw or blanket, small or large. The squares can also be made into cushions, bags, rugs, jumpers, cardigans, scarves and waistcoats. At the end of the book as well as with each pattern there are suggestions for different projects that you can use the squares for. You will also find instructions for how to assemble your squares for a nice, neat finish.

## The possibilities are endless!

The granny square has a special place in my heart and I have been developing it since 2013. Over the years that I have been crocheting squares, I have continued to find new possibilities and combinations. The abundance of variation is one of the reasons I got 'hooked' on squares. Sometimes several squares are needed to build a repeating pattern, and completely new patterns can appear just by rotating one or more of the squares in a group. A square can also reveal a completely new expression when worked with different contrasts or colour combinations.

I wish you the best of luck with exploring the squares in this book and hope that you – just like me – will find a lot of pleasure in crocheting them!

# Crochet hooks

The size (thickness) of a crochet hook can be specified in different ways. There are multiple variations, depending on factors such as whether the crochet hook is made from aluminium or steel, if it was made in Europe, the USA, the UK or Japan, or if the diameter is measured in millimetres (which is the standard in the UK). If you stick with millimetres, the sizing will be the same no matter what the hook is made of.

# Stitches

## Abbreviations

| | |
|---|---|
| st | stitch |
| rnd | round |
| lp | loop |
| ch | chain stitch |
| ch sp | chain space |
| sl st | slip stitch |
| dc | double crochet (US single crochet) |
| tr | treble crochet (US double crochet) |
| htr | half treble crochet (US half double crochet) |
| dtr | double treble crochet (US treble crochet) |
| cl | cluster |
| yo | yarn over |

## Yarn over

A yarn over is when you catch the yarn with the crochet hook. This is done to pull it through one or more stitches, to create another loop on the hook, or to make taller stitches like treble crochets. You can see a yarn over in the first illustration opposite.

Asterisks (*) mark sections in the pattern that are to be repeated a set number of times. For example: 'Work *1 dc, 1 ch, miss 1 st*, repeat * to * until end of rnd.' Repeat the instructions between the asterisks until you reach the end of the round.

## Magic Ring

Make a ring at the end of your yarn. It's important that the tail end of the yarn sits underneath where the yarn crosses over. Hold the ring with your thumb and index finger (marked with a red circle). Insert the crochet hook into the ring and make a yarn over with the ball end of the yarn; then pull it through the ring.

Now you have a first, loose loop on your crochet hook. Yarn over again with the ball end of the yarn, pulling the yarn through the loop. Now you can start crocheting stitches around the ring, following the pattern. Pull the tail end of the yarn to close the ring. You can start your squares with a magic ring.

## Chain stitch (ch)

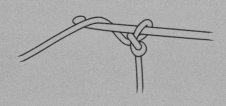 

First, make a slipknot. Insert the crochet hook into the loop and tighten the yarn around the crochet hook (but not too tightly). Yarn over with the ball end of the yarn (as opposed to the tail end) and pull a loop through the slipknot. You've just made a chain stitch. Many crochet projects start with a chain of stitches called a foundation chain. To do this, simply make chain stitches until you have the required amount.

When you crochet into a foundation chain, i.e. on the first round, there are two ways to insert the crochet hook into the loops. You can either insert the hook so there are two loops from the chain stitch over it and one under (this makes the first round a bit thicker and less elastic), or you can insert it so that one loop from the chain stitch sits over the crochet hook and two under (this makes the first round thinner but more elastic). If they are slip stitched together to form a ring, work the first round's stitches into the ring, as with a magic ring.

Chain stitches can start a project or be used within a pattern. One or several chain stitches in a row create a gap called a chain space (ch sp).

## Slip stitch (sl st)

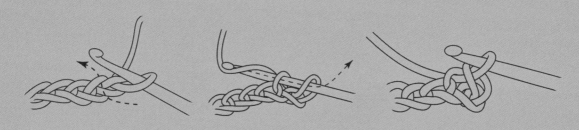

Insert the hook into a stitch, yarn over and pull the yarn through both the stitch and the loop on the hook. Insert the hook into the next stitch and continue to the end of the round. Finish with one ch to start the next round.

Slip stitches can be used to close a round by sl st into the top of the turning ch at the start of the round; you can work a whole round in sl st; or you can sl st to move your work from one area to another. They can also make a nice border, as well as make a braided chain if you work two colours, changing colours for each sl st.

## Double crochet (dc) (US single crochet)

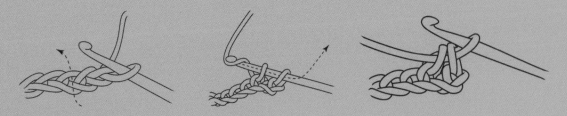

Insert the hook into a stitch, yarn over and pull a loop through. Now you have 2 loops on the hook. Yarn over again and pull through both loops on the hook at once. Insert the hook into the next stitch and continue until the end of the round. Finish with 2 chain stitches (these count as the first dc stitch on the next round) and turn. Dc stitches can be made differently: by inserting the hook through both loops of the stitch, only the back loop, only the front loop, or alternating between front and back. The work will look different depending which method you use.

## Half treble crochet (htr) (US half double crochet)

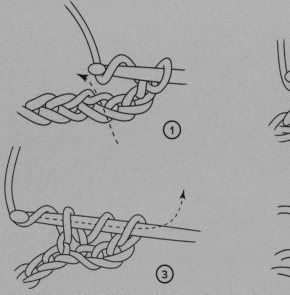
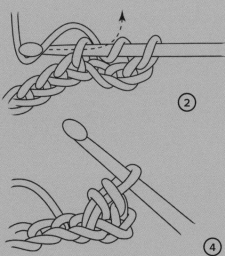
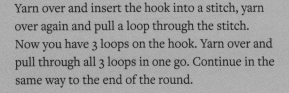

Yarn over and insert the hook into a stitch, yarn over again and pull a loop through the stitch. Now you have 3 loops on the hook. Yarn over and pull through all 3 loops in one go. Continue in the same way to the end of the round.

Finish with 3 chain stitches (these count as the first half treble stitch on the next round) to start the next round.

# Treble crochet (tr) (US double crochet)

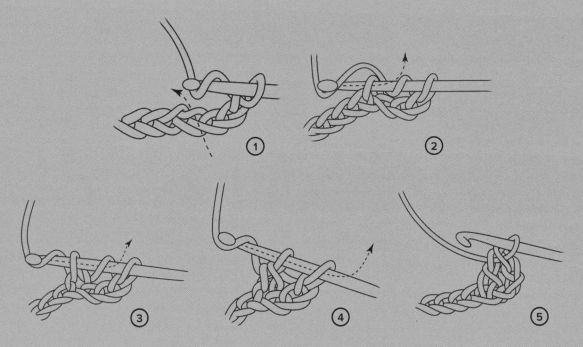

Yarn over, insert the hook into a stitch, yarn over again and pull a loop through the stitch. Now you have 3 loops on the hook. Yarn over and pull through the first two loops. Now you have 2 loops on the hook. Yarn over one final time and pull through the 2 loops. Continue in the same way to the end of the round. Finish the round with 3 chain stitches (as these count as the first treble on the next round) to start the next round. These 3 chain stitches are known as the turning chain.

---

# Double treble crochet (dtr) (US treble crochet)

Yarn over twice and insert the hook into a stitch. Yarn over again and pull a loop through the stitch. Now you have 4 loops on the hook. Yarn over and pull through the first 2 loops (3 loops left on hook), yarn over again and pull through the first 2 loops (2 loops left on hook), yarn over one final time and pull through the last 2 loops. Continue in this way to the end of the round. Finish the round with 4 chain stitches (these count as the first double treble on the next round) to start the next round.

All dtr crochet stitches start with two yarn overs. When you crochet double, treble or quadruple treble stitches and so on, you build on the treble crochet stitch. The number of initial yos determines the height of the stitch. A triple treble stitch starts with three yos, a quadruple treble stitch with four yos and so on. Always pull the yarn through 2 loops at a time until only 1 stitch remains on the hook.

# Clusters (cl)

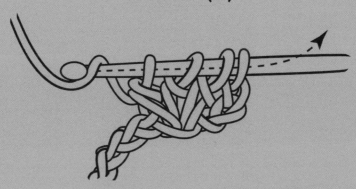

The number of treble crochet stitches in a cluster depends on the pattern. Clusters with more treble stitches become bobble or popcorn stitches. In the illustration above, a 3 treble cluster is worked into the same stitch (4th from the hook of the foundation chain), but only up to (and including) the second to last loop. Once the required number of stitches are worked this way, yarn over and pull through all the loops, finishing all 3 stitches together.

Work as follows: yo, insert hook into appropriate st/ch sp, yo and pull through. Yo and pull through 2 (leaving 2 loops on the hook for the first tr). Repeat twice more until there are 4 loops on the hook, then yo and pull through all 4 loops.

Because clusters are wide, you will usually leave a gap of at least one stitch between them. Once a cluster is done, make a chain stitch. Miss the next stitch so there is one space between clusters. Yarn over, insert the hook into the next stitch and continue the same way until the end of the round. Finish the round with 3 chain stitches and turn.

## Spike stitch

This is a double crochet stitch, but the hook is inserted further down in the work, meaning that you go over one or several rounds.

## Long treble crochet

This is a treble crochet stitch but the hook is inserted further down into the work (similar to the spike stitch.) Yarn over and insert the hook two rounds further down (i.e. skip one round and crochet into the previous round) only in the front loop and finish working the treble crochet as normal. This will be used for mosaic crochet.

## Colour change

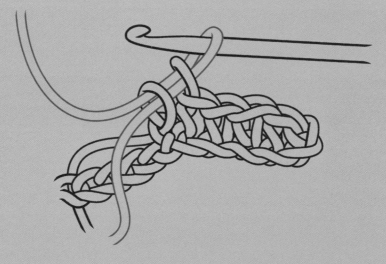

Change colour in the last yarn over of a stitch. Work stitch as normal, but when you get to the last yarn over use the new colour of yarn to complete the stitch.

## Finishing the work

Cut the yarn leaving a tail of about 15cm after completing the last stitch. Pull the yarn end through the loop and pull tight. Darn in the loose end.

## Turning

When you have crocheted a full round, you need to crochet a few chain stitches to 'get up to the height' of the next round. This is known as the turning chain, and the number of chain stitches to make depends on which stitches you will be using for the next round. The chain stitches generally count as the first stitch on the next round. The table to the right shows how many extra chain stitches you need when turning.

Each chart clearly shows the number of chain stitches required. Most squares are worked in the round from the right side throughout, but sometimes you need to turn the work to crochet the next round.

| Type of stitch | Number of chain stitches |
|---|---|
| slip stitch | 1 |
| double crochet (US single crochet) | 2 |
| half treble crochet (US half double crochet) | 3 |
| treble crochet (US double crochet) | 3 |
| double treble crochet (US treble crochet) | 4 |

# Tips and tricks

**Tension** (gauge) refers to how tightly or loosely you crochet – I crochet tightly, but everyone is different. If you notice that your squares end up larger than sizes stated in the patterns, you can try using a smaller crochet hook. If you notice that your squares end up smaller, change to a larger crochet hook. Or crochet sample squares with your own tension and measure them when you're planning your projects.

**Yardage** is difficult to estimate for individual squares; they weigh so little. An average granny square weighs 5–6 grams. Start by weighing the balls of yarn you want to use. When you have crocheted enough squares to create a section of, for example, a pattern repeat, weigh your yarn balls again. Now you know how much yarn is needed for one repeat of squares and can work out how much you'll need for your project. Don't forget borders and yarn for crocheting or sewing your project together. It's always good to allow for an extra bit of yarn.

**Crocheting with two colours per round** can seem a little awkward at first. For classic granny squares you can crochet over the yarn you're not using. Place the yarn you're not working with along the previous round, preferably slightly angled downwards diagonally to minimise the risk of it becoming visible. Weave it in by crocheting around it. You might need to pull the yarn not being worked on along the round a little to prevent it from hanging loose on the wrong side of the work. This is particularly important over longer distances. If the yarn is still showing, you can, when working the next round, insert the hook underneath it and crochet it in place, for example when working the 3 tr that are crocheted in the current ch sp.

**Yarn tangles** can easily happen when you crochet with two colours per round. The strands wrap around each other as you change colours several times during the same round. A simple tip for untangling the yarns is to hold one ball in each hand and let the square hang in the air so that the threads untangle themselves.

**Crocheting with one colour per round** is easy. The yarn that is not being worked is left aside at the start/end of the round as you work the round and is picked back up again for the next round, when the other colour is then left aside. When you crochet with one colour per round the square is thinner and more flexible than if you crochet with two colours per round. It also uses less yarn.

**Stitch markers** will help you keep track of the start/end of a round. In the charts, all rounds begin with a turning chain that corresponds to the height of the first stitch on the round and sometimes a stitch marker in the last chain stitch can be helpful so that you know where to insert the hook to finish the round with a slip stitch. Move the stitch marker for every round.

**To change colour for a new round,** first work the round you are on until you are about to make the sl st to close the round. Put the hook into the top of the stitch/turning chain in the usual way, but instead of pulling through the working yarn, pull through your second colour to finish the slip stitch. Your second colour is now on the hook, ready to begin the new round.

**Cut the yarn** when you see from the chart that the colour isn't used anymore, or if there are several rounds until the yarn is used again, remembering to leave enough of a tail to darn in. A simple rule is to cut the yarn if there are more than two rounds until you need to use it again. If there's only one round between, you don't need to cut the yarn. Instead, follow the method given left.

This hexagon is called Torild (see p. 95.)

Daisy p. 107

Dainty p. 110

# GRANNY SQUARES

The granny square is a much-loved classic. As early as 1891, it can be found pictured in the book *The Art of Crocheting,* published by the Butterick Publishing Co,. and there are many variations. Most squares in this book use the granny square as a base and I have been developing it for many years so that it can form patterns in many different ways. A repeat pattern can be made by putting several squares together. Here are a few of them!

# How to read crochet charts

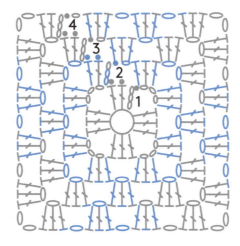

A chart accompanies each design in this book, showing which stitches you should crochet for each round, and when to change colours. Numbers indicate which round it is, borders are not numbered. Each stitch has its own symbol, and opposite you'll see the key to what those symbols mean.

When using slip stitches to get to the right place or to start the next round, slip stitch into the top of the turning chain for that round in order to complete it. This slip stitch isn't always included in the charts, but just remember that you should slip stitch your way to the place where you want to start the turning chain of the next round, and it will be correct.

# Key to symbols

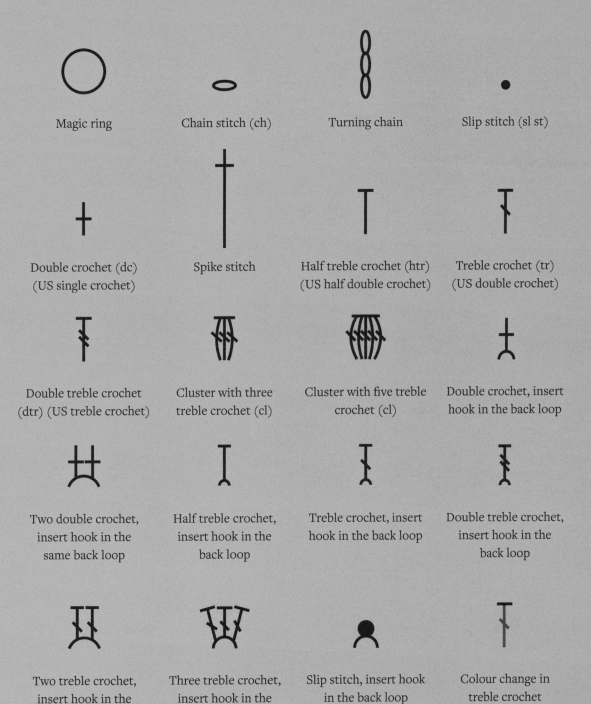

# Fighter

*This is a classic granny square with black and white edges, which gives it a three-dimensional feel. There are also a few basic squares that show how to vary the granny square. Use the black and white edge to finish any square you want.*

**Level:** Easy
**Square size:** 8.5 × 8.5cm
**Yarn:** 2-ply wool yarn
**Crochet hook:** 2.5mm or size needed to obtain tension
**Colours:** Any number of colours plus 2 colours (black and white) for the edges of each square

Start by making a magic ring for a closed centre, or work 6 ch and join with sl st in first ch to form a ring.

Follow chart 1 on p. 22 or choose one of the other versions on p. 23 in charts 2–6.

# Charts: Fighter (1–6)

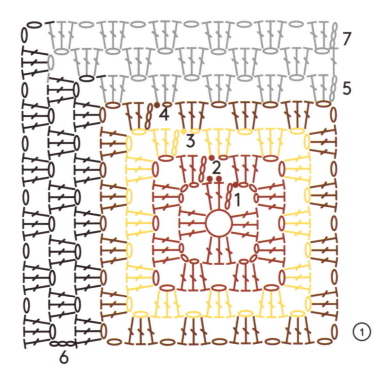

**The edge**

When crocheting the black and white edges around the square, work in rows back and forth – that is, you turn the work and crochet the other way rather than in rounds.

Change colour in the corner ch sp and leave behind the working yarn, continuing with the other colour. For the even rounds, place the yarn you aren't using aside at the front of the work (towards you). For odd rounds place the yarn you aren't using at the back of the work.

**Assembly**

Crochet the squares together in the last round. Start the last round for your second square in white yarn with 3 ch (counts as first tr) and work 1 dc into the opposite square's corner ch sp. Work 2 tr into the current square's ch sp. Continue crocheting the squares together according to the basic principle (see 'Assembly' chapter on p. 164). With white work 3 tr in the corner ch sp. Crochet 1 dc in the opposite top square's corner ch sp and work 1 dc into the ch sp on the opposite left square (the third square). Change colour to black and continue following the instructions. Finish the round with 3 tr in the last corner ch sp and 1 dc in the opposite square's corner ch sp.

GRANNY SQUARES 23

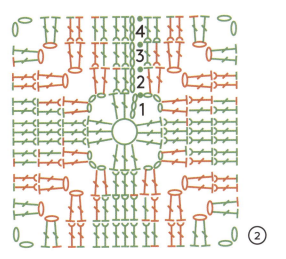

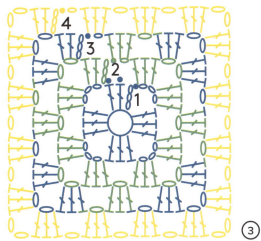

Chart 2: Most treble crochets are worked in the back loop only, while stitches worked into ch sps are worked over the full chain. This is to create a softer transition in the pattern.

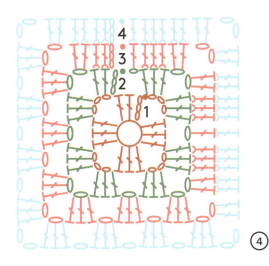

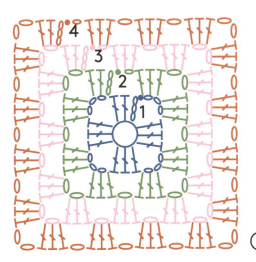

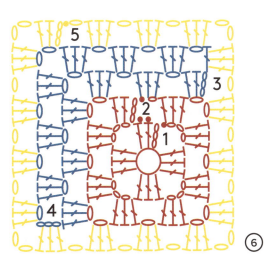

# Ulla-Bella

*I've taken inspiration from vintage textiles for this square. I have put together several squares into lengths and crocheted a border with bobbles along the long sides. The lengths can become the hem for a jumper – or several squares can become a blanket with a border.*

**Level:** Easy
**Square size:** 8 × 8cm
**Yarn:** 2-ply wool yarn
**Crochet hook:** 2.5mm or size needed to obtain tension
**Colours:** 4 colours per square, plus 2 colours for the border (black + 1 colour for the bobbles)

Start by making a magic ring for a closed centre, or work 6 ch and sl st in first ch to form a ring.

Follow the chart on p. 26.

Work the last round of the border with the bobbles from the wrong side of the work. This will make the bobbles 'pop' out on the right side. Bobbles are essentially big clusters (see p. 12), so follow the instructions for a cluster stitch, but replace 3 tr stitches with 5, ultimately drawing the yarn through 6 hook stitches.

# Chart: Ulla-Bella

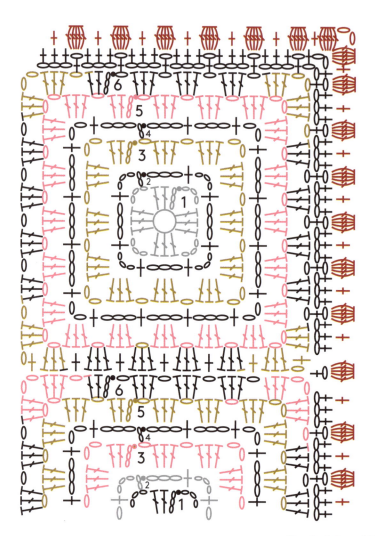

The chart shows 1 ½ squares plus parts of the border. The two squares are identical, apart from the colour order.

**Project suggestions**

*Braces:* Crochet squares to the required length, assemble and crochet the border with bobbles along both long sides. Braces can look nice added to a skirt and paired with a blouse or a t-shirt. Secure the braces in place with buttons or clips.

*Cushion:* Crochet lengths with the border along all sides and sew to the backing for a cushion cover, or crochet squares to create a cushion cover. For example, 36 squares arranged 6 x 6 make a cover that measures 48 × 48cm. With the border the cover will measure approx. 50cm.

# Brother Roger

*This square is perfect for a small child's blanket or cushions. Or try making your own bag!*

---

**Level:** Easy
**Square size:** 8 × 8cm
**Yarn:** 2–ply wool yarn
**Crochet hook:** 2.5mm or size needed to obtain tension
**Colours:** 1 main colour for the squares (white), plus 6 accent colours

---

Start by making a magic ring for a closed centre, or work 6 ch and sl st in first ch to form a ring.

Choose which square you want to crochet and follow the chart.

# Charts: Brother Roger (1–2)

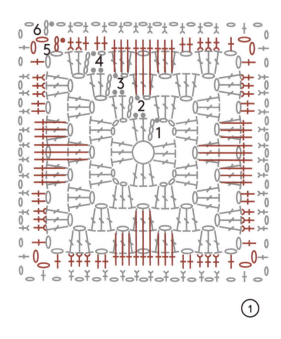

①

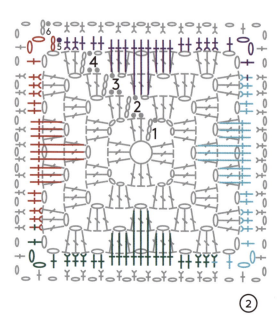

②

Chart 1 starts by crocheting a single-coloured, standard granny square for 4 rounds and then change to the second round to work round 5. Make a final round in the main colour so that you can crochet the squares together as you go along.

Chart 2 shows that the spike stitch colours that make up round 5 are different for each side. Cut the colour after completing each one.

### Assembly
The squares can either be assembled diagonally so that the main colour of the square forms a cross, or you can assemble them side by side so that the main colour forms an X. I have assembled my squares diagonally so that the work gets a 'jagged' edge.

**Project suggestions**

*Cushion:* crochet squares to required width and length – 36 squares arranged 6 × 6 will make a cushion measuring 48 × 48cm.

*Bag:* crochet a bag with squares that are assembled side by side, not diagonally. For a rectangular bag 40cm wide and 48cm high, join squares to make a rectangle 5 squares wide and 6 high for each side of the bag (30 squares per side).

*Blanket:* I have assembled my squares diagonally to get a jagged edge, so the main colour forms a cross pattern. For a child's blanket measuring 79 × 113cm you will need 70 squares arranged 7 × 10.

GRANNY SQUARES 29

# Lollipop

*The round circle in the middle is based on vintage crocheted potholders, and the edge around the circle is worked like a granny square. The lollipops stand out from the darker background, which gives a fun, graphic depth to the pattern.*

**Level:** Advanced

**Square size:** 15.5 × 15.5cm

**Yarn:** 2-/3-ply cotton yarn

**Crochet hook:** 2.5mm or size needed to obtain tension

**Colours:** 5–8 colours (2 for each lollipop swirl, 1 for the centres, 3 for the background and border)

Start by making a magic ring for a closed centre, or work 6 ch and sl st to first ch to form a ring.

Follow the chart on p. 33.

# Chart: Lollipop

The chart shows a white and red swirl in the middle with light blue along two of the sides.

To make the white and blue swirl, swap the red for blue and make sure to crochet the light blue stitches on the last round (round 13) in two diagonally opposite corners.

The two rounds of the edging are shown on the top and left-hand edges of the chart. The last light blue round includes spike stitches that go down two rounds and sit on the right side of the work.

**Assembly**
Crochet the squares together as and when they're finished.

Crochet the border around the whole work.

**First round of the border:** work double crochet in the back loops only of the stitches of the previous round or into the ch sps.

**Second round of the border:** work the dcs in the back loops only and long trs in the front loops only on round 13. The long treble crochet stitches are worked as follows: yo and insert the hook into the front loop on round 13 so that the yarn sits on top of round 14. Finish working the treble crochet so that it comes up to the current round you're working on.

**Project suggestions**
*Cushion:* for a cushion measuring 62 × 62cm you will need 16 squares arranged 4 × 4. For a rectangular cushion measuring 31 × 62cm you will need 8 squares arranged 2 × 4. You can decorate the cushion with red pompoms in the corners - see how to make pompoms on p. 40.

*Child's blanket:* for a blanket measuring 77.5 × 108.5cm you will need 35 squares arranged 5 × 7.

*Bag:* for a bag measuring 31 × 31 cm you will need 4 squares arranged 2 × 2 for the front panel. Assemble the squares and sew together with a back panel of leather or wool. Line the bag. Crochet a handle: 10 ch and work dc rows through both loops to make it sturdy. Crochet to length of your choice and sew onto the bag.

GRANNY SQUARES 33

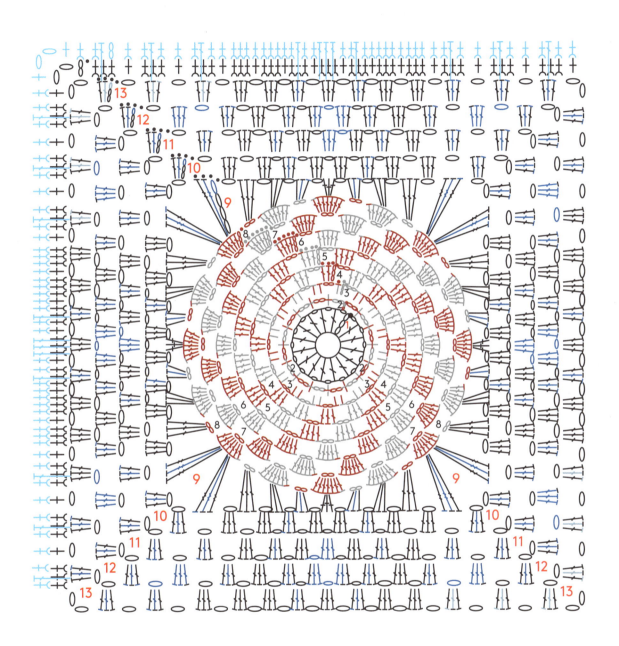

# Twist

*The round granny square is again based on vintage crochet potholders. Here I wanted to create a dynamic movement in the Escher-like pattern. The twist changes direction at the edges, and the beige and black colours enhance the graphic pattern.*

**Level:** Fairly easy
**Circle Size:** 11.5 × 11.5cm
**Square size:** 3.5 × 3.5cm
**Yarn:** 4-ply cotton yarn
**Crochet hook:** 2.5mm or size needed to obtain tension
**Colours:** 2 (black and beige)

Start by making a magic ring for a closed centre, or work 6 ch and sl st to first ch to form a ring.

For a full pattern repeat you will need 4 circles and one whole square.

Follow charts 1–3 on pp. 36-37.

## Charts: Twist (1–3)

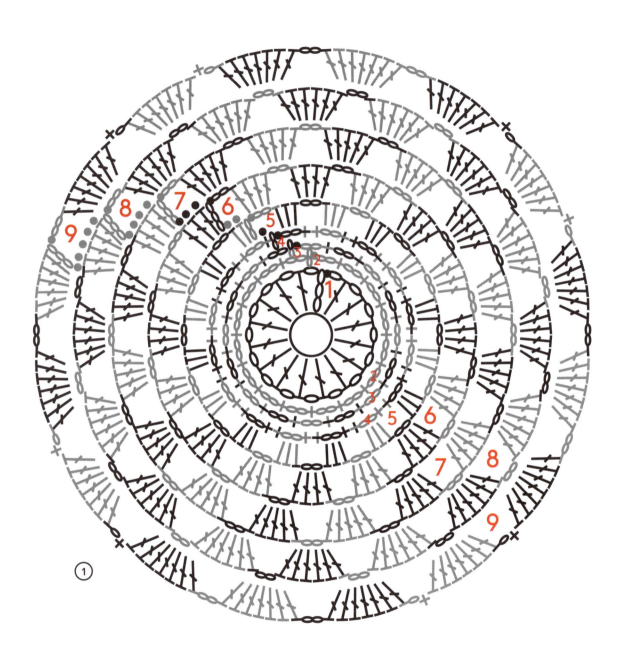

①

# GRANNY SQUARES

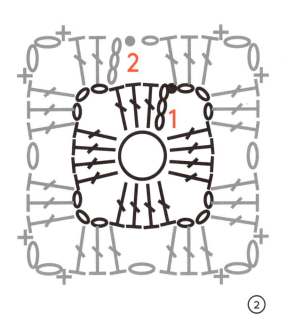

②

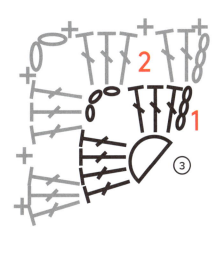

③

Chart 1 is a circle, and the dc at the edge shows where to crochet them together with the other circles – see lower edge of the sample on p. 34.

Chart 2 is for the squares that sit between the circles. The dc at the edges shows where to crochet them together with the circles.

Chart 3 is half a square, and the dc at the edge shows where to crochet it together with the circles. This is an optional variation.

**Assembly**
Crochet the circles/squares together as you go. Start by joining the circles. 4 of the 7 tr stitch groups are flanked by a dc stitch and the circles should be joined in the centre stitch of these 7 tr groups. Ch 1 then 1 dc in the centre tr of the 7 tr group. Now work 1 dc in the corresponding centre tr of the next circle. When you have crocheted 4 circles together, crochet the square in the middle of the circles, this time attaching the squares at the corner spaces.

If you want your projects to have straight edges rather than scalloped edges you also need to crochet the half squares from chart 3, as they will fill in the gaps. Do this when all circles and squares are assembled for best result.

**Project suggestions**
Blanket or rug in a thicker yarn.

# Pillerull

*This is a good project for using up leftover yarn! It is based on two squares, one in a checked pattern of black and another colour, and the other mainly black. I have assembled the squares into a little blanket and added pompoms to the outer edges.*

**Level:** Easy with colour changes on some rounds
**Square size:** 8 × 8cm
**Yarn:** 2–ply wool yarn
**Crochet hook:** 2.5mm or size needed to obtain tension
**Colours:** As many colours as you want with 1 main colour (black), that you will need more of

Start by making a magic ring for a closed centre or work 6 ch and sl st to first ch to form a ring.

Follow the charts on p. 41.

# Charts: Pillerull (1–2)

Chart 1 is a checked square with 1 colour plus main colour (in this case, black).

Chart 2 is a square in the main colour with 1 colour in the middle and 2 more colours in diagonally opposite corners.

For the sections with different colours in the corners of rounds 4 and 5 on chart 2, cut a 125cm length of each colour. Crochet from the middle of the yarn on round 4 and use the beginning of the yarn for round 5. Hold the yarn for round 5 slightly looser when you continue crocheting with the yarn (second half) at the beginning of the round.

**Pompom**
Cut out two circle templates from sturdy cardboard, slightly larger in diameter than you want the pompom to be. Make a good-sized hole in the middle. Thread yarn onto a darning needle then wrap the yarn tightly through the hole and around the cardboard discs so that the yarn covers the carboard completely. The more you wrap the yarn around, the fuller and fluffier the pompom will be. When you have finished, cut the yarn along the outside edge. Carefully slot a thread that is stronger than wool yarn (for example cotton or linen) in between the carboard discs and tie the thread together. Remove the carboard, and now you have a round pompom. Trim as needed so it is even. You can steam it in a (metal) colander over boiling water to make it nice and full.

Sew pompoms to the outer corner of every other square and 2 pompoms to the corner squares.

**Assembly of small blanket**
Crochet the squares together using the photographs below and on p. 38 as a placement guide. The squares in the photograph below are numbered in the order in which they are worked and joined.

1a – chart 1 and the first square to be crocheted.

1b, c, d, and e – chart 1 and are the four squares which are crocheted together with 1a.

2 – chart 1 (same colours for the whole blanket) and the first edge square for the outer edges.

3a, b, c and d – chart 2. Squares 3c and 3d have white corners.

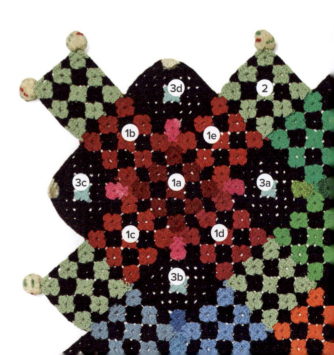

GRANNY SQUARES 41

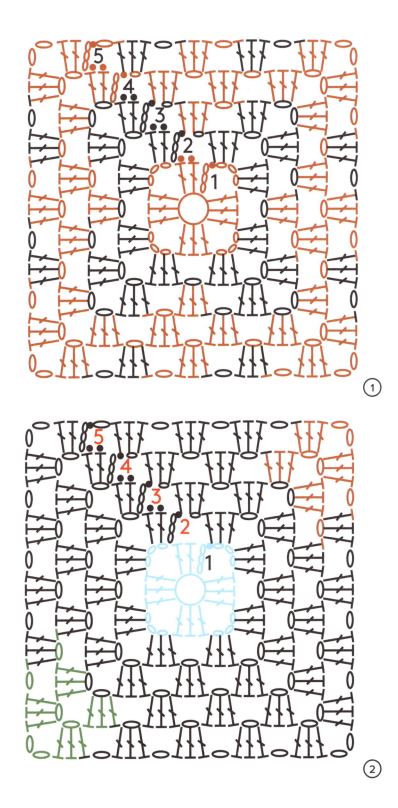

# Tora

*By changing colours in the 3 treble groups, you will achieve different effects that create a unique pattern. The more often you vary the colours of the treble stitches, the more intricate the pattern becomes.*

**Level:** Intermediate
**Square size:** 7 × 7cm
**Yarn:** 2-/3-ply cotton yarn
**Crochet hook:** 2.5mm or size needed to obtain tension
**Colours:** 2 (black and white)

The wrong side will be just as nice as the right side, since there aren't any 'floats' on the reverse when crocheting a standard granny square. This is because of the colour changes that are made in the treble crochet groups (1 black tr, 1 white tr, 1 black tr).

Start by making a magic ring for a closed centre or work 6 ch and sl st to first ch to form a ring.

Follow the chart on p. 44.

## Chart: Tora

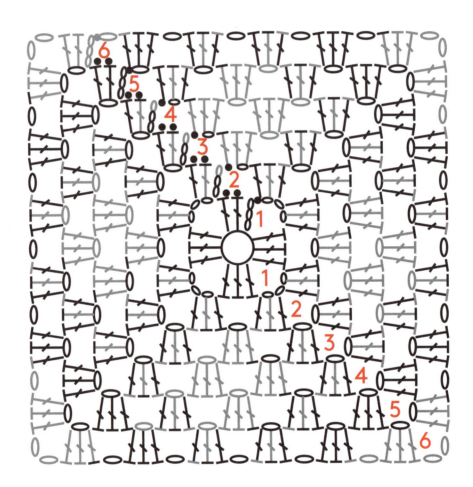

**Project suggestions**
The squares can be used for clothes, a blanket, a cushion or a bag – or why not a small rug using thicker yarn?

# Waldemar

*The inspiration for this square came from a woven pattern.*

**Level:** Easy
**Square size:** 9 × 9cm
**Yarn:** 2-ply wool yarn
**Crochet hook:** 2.5mm or size needed to obtain tension
**Colours:** 3

Start by making a magic ring for a closed centre or work 6 ch and sl st to first ch to form a ring.

Follow the chart on p. 47.

# Chart: Waldemar

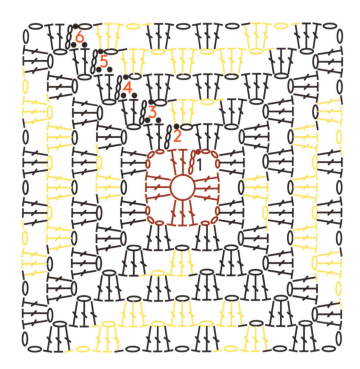

Cut the yarn after round 1 since that colour is only worked in this round.

Round 4 is worked in one colour only. Leave aside the second colour from round 3 when working round 4. Then finish round 4 by bringing the second colour up to the level of the current round. Place the crochet hook underneath the yarn and make the slip stitch that finishes the round. This binds the yarn and brings it up to the right level for the next round (round 5).

### Project suggestions
A blanket, cushion, or small rug to have by the bed. You can also cover a pouffe with this pattern!

# Agda

*The Agda square is a slightly easier version of the Hilda square (p. 51) which, among other things, uses more colour. I have been inspired by woven patterns for both squares.*

**Level:** Easy if you are used to colour changes
**Square size:** 5.5 × 5.5cm
**Yarn:** 2-/3-ply cotton yarn
**Crochet hook:** 2.5mm or size needed to obtain tension
**Colours:** 2

The wrong side will be just as nice as the right side since there aren't any 'floats' on the reverse because the colour changes are made in the treble crochet groups.

Start by making a magic ring for a closed centre or work 6 ch and sl st to first ch to form a ring.

Follow the chart on p. 50.

# Chart: Agda

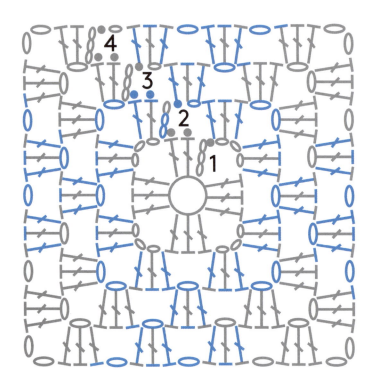

**Project suggestions**

*Vest*: see chart on p. 160.

*Ladies' jumper*: see chart on p. 161.

*Waistcoat or slipover*: see chart on p. 163.

*Child's blanket*: for a blanket measuring 71.5 × 110cm you will need 260 squares arranged 13 × 20.

# Hilda

*This is slightly more complicated to crochet than the Agda square (p. 48) because on round 3 you are crocheting with three colours!*

**Level:** Intermediate as round 3 is worked with 3 colours and is slightly more complicated to crochet
**Square size:** 5.5 × 5.5cm
**Yarn:** 2-/3-ply cotton yarn
**Crochet hook:** 2.5mm or size needed to obtain tension
**Colours:** 3

The wrong side will be just as nice as the right side since there aren't any 'floats' on the reverse because the colour changes are made in the treble crochet groups.

Start by making a magic ring for a closed centre or work 6 ch and sl st to first ch to form a ring.

Follow the chart on p. 52.

## Chart: **Hilda**

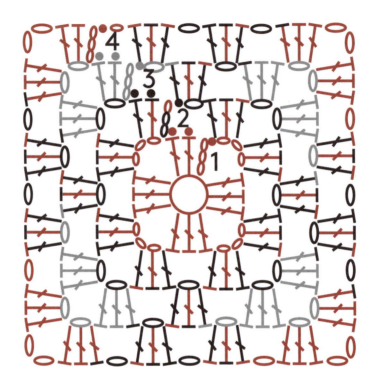

Cut the grey yarn after round 3 since it is only worked in this round.

**Project suggestions**

*Vest*: see chart on p. 160.

*Ladies' jumper*: see chart on p. 161.

*Waistcoat or slipover*: see chart on p. 163.

*Small bag*: for a bag measuring 22 × 22cm you will need 16 squares arranged 4 × 4 for the front panel. Then crochet 16 single-coloured squares for the back panel. Assemble the squares and line the bag. Crochet a handle: work 5 ch and dc in rows through both loops to make it sturdy. Work to the length of your choice and sew onto the bag. Sew in a zip or snap button at the opening.

# Dialogue

*This square and the Delight square (p. 58) are built on the same principle and base pattern but have completely different expressions. The last three rounds are what set them apart.*

**Level:** Easy but the pattern in the corners of the square require colour changes

**Square size:** 12 × 12cm

**Yarn:** 2-/3-ply wool yarn

**Crochet hook:** 2.5mm or size needed to obtain tension

**Colours:** 4 (beige, black, blue, red)

The wrong side is just as nice as the right side.

Start by making a magic ring for a closed centre or work 6 ch and sl st to first ch to form a ring.

Follow charts 1 and 2 on pp. 56-57.

## Charts: Dialogue (1–2)

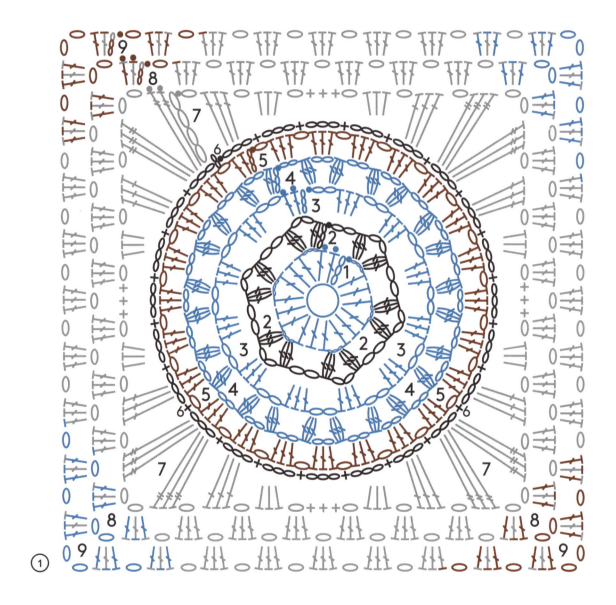

I have varied the colours to create two different base squares, shown in charts 1 and 2.

When you have finished with a colour that is coming back later in the square, you get the best result by cutting the yarn and joining it again when the colour next appears in the chart.

Every other corner is worked in blue and red yarn. Cut a 150cm length of yarn of each colour and start crocheting from the middle of the yarn for round 8, and then continue with the other half on round 9. Hold the yarn slightly looser when you continue using it at the beginning of round 9.

GRANNY SQUARES

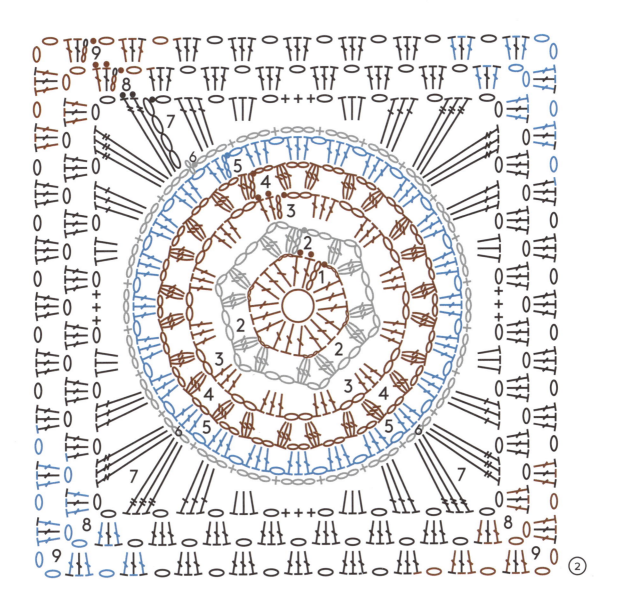

**Project suggestions**

*Shawl*: see chart on p. 162.

*Blanket*: for a blanket measuring 120 × 156cm you will need 130 squares arranged 10 × 13.

*Cushion*: for a cushion measuring 60 × 60cm you will need 25 squares arranged 5 × 5 for the front panel. Assemble the squares and sew together with a back panel of wool or leather.

# Delight

*I have taken inspiration for this square from old Scanian textiles in rich colours. It is built on the same principle and base pattern as the Dialogue square, but the colours give it a very different expression.*

**Level:** Advanced as the first 6 rounds are easy but after that there are a lot of colour changes

**Square size:** 12 × 12cm

**Yarn:** 4-ply or less wool yarn

**Crochet hook:** 2.5mm or size needed to obtain tension

**Colours:** 4–5 colours per square

The wrong side will be just as nice as the right side since there aren't any 'floats' on the reverse because the colour changes are made in the treble crochet groups.

Start by making a magic ring for a closed centre or work 6 ch and sl st to first ch to form a ring.

Follow charts 1 and 2 on pp. 60 and 61.

# Charts: Delight (1–2)

Chart 1 is the whole square. If you want the colours as pictured on p. 58, vary the colours in the squares as follows:

*Round 1:* Red, turquoise or yellow.

*Round 2:* Black.

*Round 3:* Same colour as round 1.

*Round 4–5:* Black.

*Round 6:* Every other square in turquoise or red.

*Round 7:* If turquoise was used in round 6, use red here and vice versa.

*Round 8:* Use black plus the same colour used for round 6.

*Round 9:* Use black plus the same colour for all squares, following the chart.

Chart 2 shows how to further vary the colours in rounds 1–3. Work rounds 2–3 in green or white. The rest of the square is worked following chart 1.

Crochet the squares together as you go.

**Project suggestions**
This square works well for a blanket or cushion, or try making a shawl (see chart on p. 162) or cardigan with single-coloured sleeves.

GRANNY SQUARES

①

# Jambo

*African patterns were my inspiration for the Jambo, Aida and Acke squares. All three patterns are made up of different types of rhombi which, when grouped together in black and white, display a clear, graphic design.*

**Level:** Easy if you are used to colour changes
**Square size:** 5.5 × 5.5cm
**Yarn:** 2-/3-ply cotton yarn
**Crochet hook:** 2.5mm or size needed to obtain tension
**Colours:** 2

The wrong side is just as nice as the right side since there aren't any 'floats' on the reverse because the colour changes are made in the treble crochet groups (1 black tr, 1 white tr, 1 black tr).

Start by making a magic ring for a closed centre or work 6 ch and sl st to first ch to form a ring.

Follow the chart on p. 64.

## Chart: Jambo

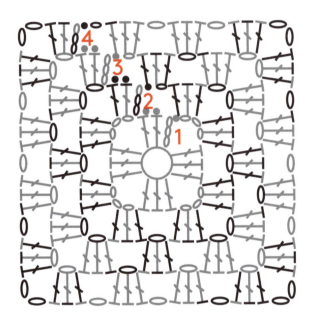

**Project suggestions**
The strong graphic patterns of the Jambo, Aida and Acke squares would work well for a blanket, cushion, bag or perhaps a straight skirt with an elastic waistband. With thicker yarn, they also work well for rugs.

*Vest*: see chart on p. 160.

*Ladies' jumper*: see chart on p. 161.

*Waistcoat or slipover*: see chart on p. 163.

# Aida

*The Aida, Acke and Jambo squares have the same basic structure but the pattern is varied by sizes and the treble crochet colour choice.*

**Level:** Intermediate
**Square size:** 6.5 × 6.5cm
**Yarn:** 2-/3-ply cotton yarn
**Crochet hook:** 2.5mm or size needed to obtain tension
**Colours:** 2

The wrong side will be just as nice as the right side since there aren't any 'floats' on the reverse because the colour changes are made in the treble crochet clusters (1 white tr, 1 black tr, 1 white tr).

Start by making a magic ring for a closed centre or work 6 ch and sl st to first ch to form a ring.

Follow the chart on p. 66.

# Chart: Aida

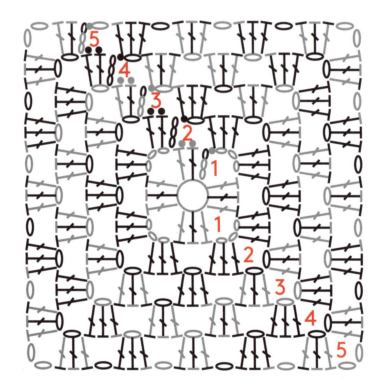

**Project suggestions**
*Waistcoat or slipover*: see chart on p. 163.

# Acke

*The Jambo, Aida and Acke squares are closely related, with Acke having the largest square of the three. Compare the three squares and experiment with changing the colours.*

**Level:** Advanced
**Square size:** 10 × 10cm
**Yarn:** 2-/3-ply cotton yarn
**Crochet hook:** 2.5mm or size needed to obtain tension
**Colours:** 2

The wrong side will be just as nice as the right side since there aren't any 'floats' on the reverse because the colour changes are made in the treble crochet groups (1 black tr, 1 white tr, 1 black tr).

Start by making a magic ring for a closed centre or work 6 ch and sl st to first ch to form a ring.

Follow the chart on p. 70.

## Chart: Acke

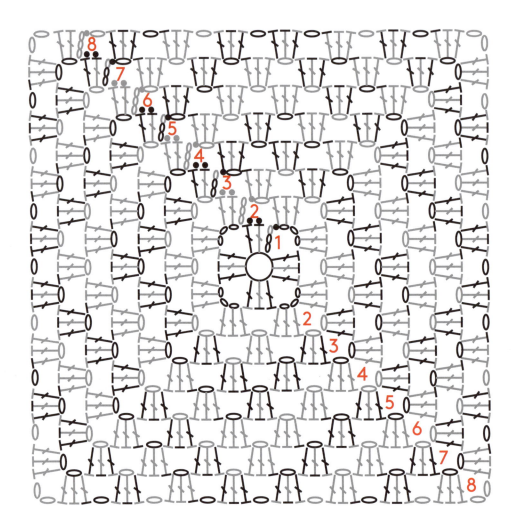

**Project suggestions**
*Long cardigan*: see chart on p. 162.

# Zola

*This square is built up the same way as the Tora square (p. 42), but the colour changes create a new pattern.*

---

**Level:** Easy, if you are used to colour changes
**Square size:** 6.5 × 6.5cm
**Yarn:** 2-/3-ply cotton yarn
**Crochet hook:** 2.5mm or size needed to obtain tension
**Colours:** 2

---

The wrong side will be just as nice as the right side since there aren't any 'floats' on the reverse because the colour changes are made in the treble crochet groups (1 black tr, 1 white tr, 1 black tr).

Start by making a magic ring for a closed centre or work 6 ch and sl st to first ch to form a ring.

Follow the chart on p. 72.

# Chart: Zola

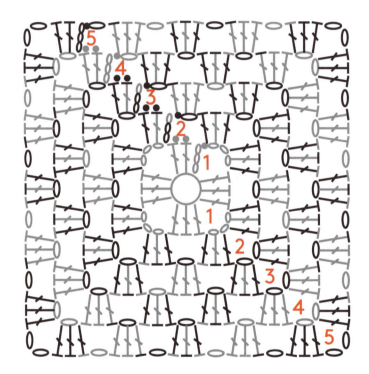

**Project suggestions**

*Waistcoat or slipover*: see chart on p. 163.

*Rug*: crochet the squares in a thicker yarn and assemble.

74 GRANNY SQUARES

# Mateo

*For this square, I was inspired by South American textiles that often are both lush and bright in their design. In the picture you can see I have made one square green and white instead of red and white. Pick your favourite colours. It's a good project for using up leftover yarn!*

**Level:** Intermediate as rounds 9–12 are worked in multiple colours and require mid-round colour changes

**Square size:** 20 × 20cm

**Yarn:** 2-ply wool yarn

**Crochet hook:** 2.5mm or size needed to obtain tension

**Colours:** As many as you like (approx. 7 colours per square)

Since round 1–8 are worked with one colour per round, the wrong side is just as nice as the right side. The multi-coloured edge (rounds 9–12) will also look nice on the wrong side.

Start by making a magic ring for a closed centre or work 6 ch and sl st to first ch to form a ring.

Follow the chart on p. 77.

# Chart: Mateo

Work rounds 1–13 and crochet the squares together on round 14.

**Assembly**
Crochet the squares together as and when they're finished.

You can crochet a border around the assembled squares.

**Border**
*Round 1*: Work as for round 13 but swap the colours (what is white on round 13 is worked in red for the first round of the border). Work dc in the back loops only, swapping the colours (red for white and white for red).

*Round 2*: Using black, dc in the back loop of each stitch. When you reach the corner sp, work 1 dc, 2 ch , 1 dc in the corner sp.

I have sewn pompoms (see how to make them on p. 40) between my squares. The pompoms I made are white and I added a colourful smaller pompom onto each. Small pompoms can also be bought from craft supply stores. Attach the white pompoms to the corners of the square first, and then sew on the colourful one.

**Project suggestions**
*Small bag (mobile phone bag)*: crochet two squares – one for the front and one for the back. Crochet a handle with double crochet working through both loops to make it sturdy. Sew in a zip if you don't want to leave the bag open.

*Blanket*: crochet a warm blanket in wool yarn. Make a version with squares that are made up of rounds 1–8 and finish the blanket with a border made up of rounds 9–12. It's a good idea to use up leftover yarn for the actual squares, but stick to two colours for the border.

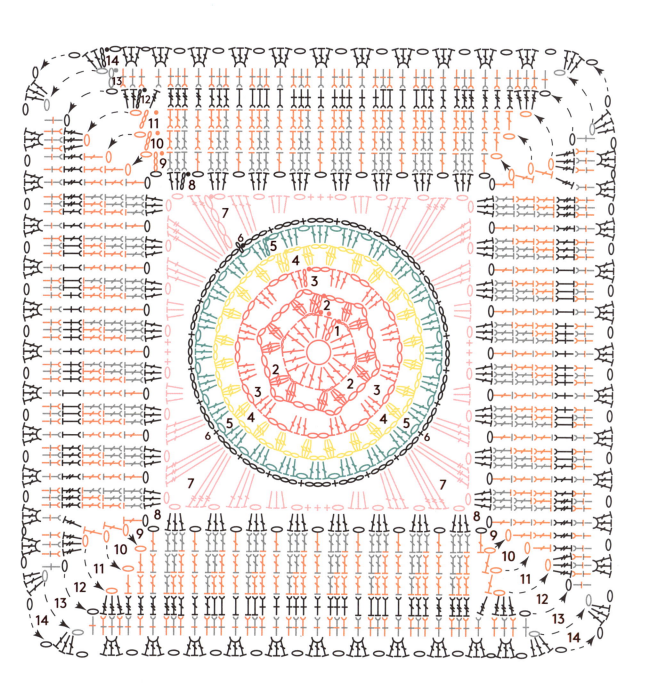

# Bahia

*Here I have been inspired by African woven baskets made from plant fibres. If you crochet with a thick yarn, one circle can become a rug. Work the first 12 rounds and you will get a smaller circle that you can make into a potholder!*

---

**Level:** Advanced

**Smaller circle**
**Circle size:** 23cm in diameter
**Yarn:** 2–/3–ply cotton yarn
**Crochet hook:** 2.5mm or size needed to obtain tension
**Colours:** 4

**Larger circle**
**Circle size:** 57cm in diameter
**Yarn:** Aran linen yarn
**Crochet hook:** 5mm or size needed to obtain tension
**Colours:** 4

---

# Chart: Bahia

Start by making a magic ring for a closed centre or work 6 ch and sl st to first ch to form a ring.

Follow the chart opposite. You can use 4 stitch markers to help you keep track, placed after each pattern repeat.

**Larger circle**
All black-and-white rounds are worked in a thicker linen yarn and those with colour (blue and red) are worked in a thinner linen yarn. Since the black-and-white rounds are worked in two colours, the yarn that is temporarily not used is carried along the round and is crocheted around. When changing colours, the other yarn is then crocheted around. The single-coloured rounds are only worked with one strand of yarn, and a second strand is not carried along the round. I have sewn small cross stiches with a thin white linen yarn in every other stitch on the second blue round (round 22) of the larger version.

**Project suggestions**
*Rug*: crochet the larger circle in a thicker yarn.

*Potholder*: crochet rounds 1–12 in a thicker cotton yarn than specified.

*Wall hanging*: crochet the larger circle in linen yarn.

GRANNY SQUARES 81

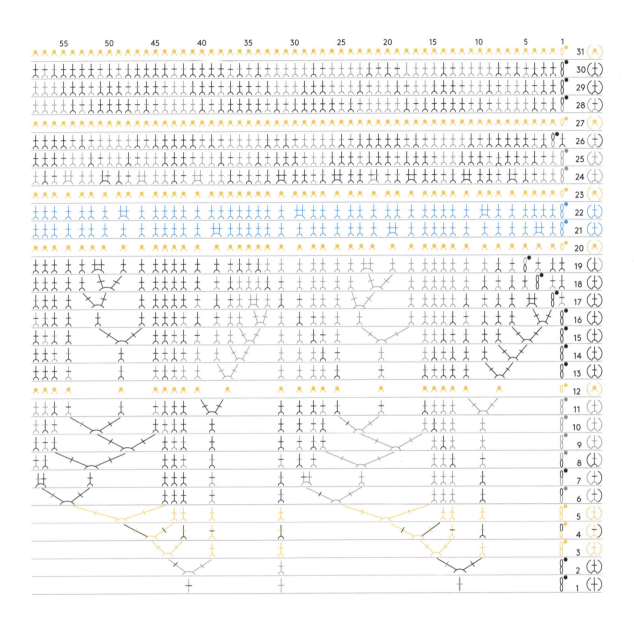

The chart shows a quarter of the circle's pattern. Crochet the chart 4 times to get the whole pattern.

At the start/end of each round the symbol for the round's first stitch is shown in brackets. This should be worked instead of the turning chain when the chart is repeated. The chain stitches are only worked at the beginning of a new round. Finish the round with a slip stitch in the second chain stitch.

Place a ruler underneath the row in the chart you're working and move it up the chart as you complete a round; it is easier to see which stitches you should work for each round this way.

# Svea

*Woven bands are the inspiration behind this square. They usually have just two colours and the pattern is often built up with intricate patterns.*

**Level:** Intermediate
**Square size:** 10 × 10cm
**Yarn:** 2-/3-ply cotton yarn
**Crochet hook:** 2.5mm or size needed to obtain tension
**Colours:** 2

The wrong side is just as nice as the right side since there aren't any 'floats' on the reverse.

Start by making a magic ring for a closed centre or work 6 ch and sl st to first ch to form a ring.

Follow the chart on p. 84.

You will need 4 squares to create a repeat pattern.

## Chart: Svea

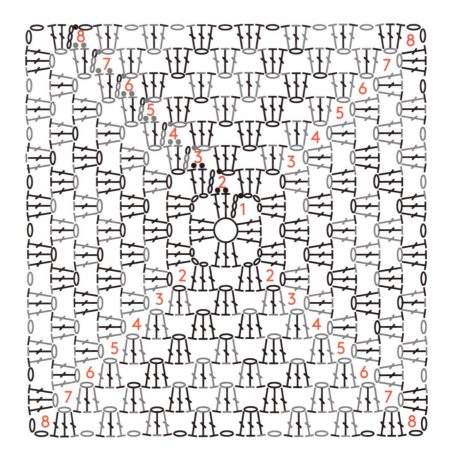

To create the two different black and white squares at the top of the next page, invert black and white in the chart. The red version shows how the pattern will look when several sets of 4 squares are put together.

**Project suggestions**
Rug in thicker yarn, blanket, cushion, braces or a long cardigan, see the chart on p. 162.

# GRANNY SQUARES

# Alfhild

*Here I was inspired by a woven pattern. If you take a closer look at different weaving techniques you can get many varied and interesting ideas for patterns.*

---

**Level:** Easy, if you are used to colour changes
**Square size:** 6 × 6cm
**Yarn:** 2-ply wool yarn
**Crochet hook:** 2.5mm or size needed to obtain tension
**Colours:** 2

---

The wrong side is just as nice as the right side since there aren't any 'floats' on the reverse thanks to the dense rounds of treble crochet, worked around the yarn not currently being used.

Start by making a magic ring for a closed centre or work 6 ch and sl st to first ch to form a ring.

Follow the chart on p. 88.

You will need 4 squares to create a repeat pattern.

# Chart: Alfhild

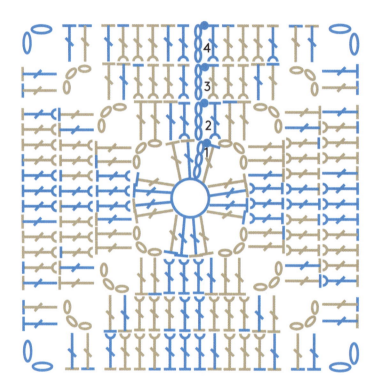

All treble crochet stitches are worked in the back loop apart from some turquoise ones that are worked through both loops – this is to get a softer transition in the pattern.

### Assembly
Crochet the squares together as and when they're finished in each corner's ch sp. Then sew the squares together from the wrong side with stitches back and forth in the outer loops of each square. With this technique the work will is almost as nice on the wrong side!

### Project suggestions
*Shawl:* For a shawl measuring 42 × 138cm you will need 161 squares arranged 7 × 23.

# Xara

*This square builds on the pattern for the square Alfhild, but Xara has more rounds and colour changes.*

**Level:** Easy, if you are used to colour changes
**Square size:** 12 × 12cm
**Yarn:** 2-ply wool yarn
**Crochet hook:** 2.5mm or size needed to obtain tensions
**Colours:** 3 per square, vary with squares in different colours

The wrong side is just as nice as the right side since there aren't any 'floats' on the reverse thanks to the dense rounds of treble crochet, worked around the yarn not currently being used.

The treble crochet stitches are worked in the back loop apart from some black ones that are worked though both loops. This is to get a softer transition in the pattern.

Start by making a magic ring for a closed centre or work 6 ch and sl st to first ch to form a ring.

Follow the chart on p. 90.

## Chart: Xara

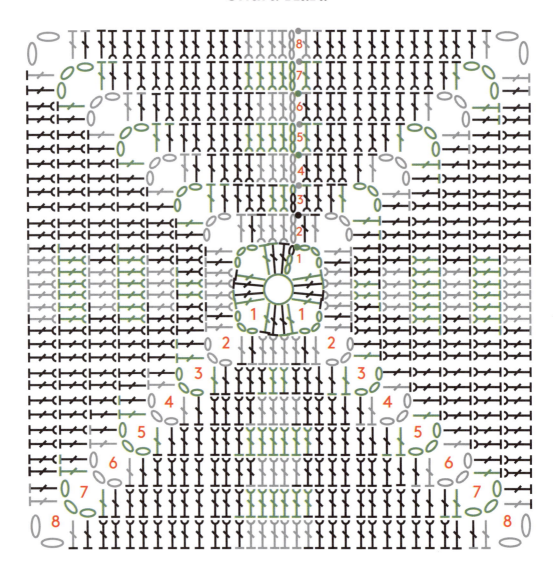

To get the variation in the squares seen opposite on p. 91, you will need 3 main colours and 3 for the vertical and diagonal bands.

The colour that you're not currently working with for the motif is left aside at the start while working the round with the other colour.

### Assembly
For a better result, block the squares one by one before joining them.

Place the squares right sides facing up, then sew them together from the wrong side in the outer loops. To tie the sections together where the pattern meets in the square's corner ch sp, I sew a small cross using a whip stitch in black yarn where 4 squares meet: 2 whip stitches going one way and 2 going the other way.

### Project suggestions
Try a blanket, cushion, bag or shawl.

# Alina

*I have always been fascinated by East Asian patterns with their intricate designs of lines and circles in a complicated symbiosis. This square is an advanced crochet project with many colours and dense colour changes.*

**Level:** Advanced
**Square size:** 11 × 11cm
**Yarn:** 2-/3-ply cotton yarn
**Crochet hook:** 2.5mm or size needed to obtain tension
**Colours:** 10 colours per square

Start by making a magic ring for a closed centre or work 6 ch and sl st to first ch to form a ring.

Follow the chart on p. 94.

# Chart: Alina

**Project suggestions**

*Cushion:* create squares to width and length of your choice. If you want, you can crochet squares for just the front panel and line the back with fabric, leather or wool.

*Bag:* crochet squares for the front panel of a bag and use wool or leather for the back.

# Torild

*These hexagons are enhanced with a last round in black to make each onestand out clearly. It's also the perfect project for cleaning out your stash of leftover yarn! Work double crochet in the back loop and turn the work after each round.*

**Level:** Easy
**Hexagon size:** 13 × 13cm
**Yarn:** 2-/3-ply cotton yarn
**Crochet hook:** 2.5mm or size needed to obtain tension
**Colours:** 2 colours per hexagon + black for the edge

The hexagons are ribbed, meaning you crochet all stitches in the back loop and turn the work after each round so that you crochet the rounds back and forth. All odd rounds are worked from the right side and all even rounds are worked from the wrong side.

Since the hexagons are crocheted with 2 colours, one colour will become dominant on one side and the other on the other side. This is an exciting and perhaps surprising effect in a blanket, for example!

Start by making a magic ring for a closed centre or work 6 ch and sl st to first ch to form a ring.

Follow the chart on p. 96. Here you can use 6 stitch markers to help you keep track, placed after each repeat of the chart (see p. 14).

# Chart: Torild

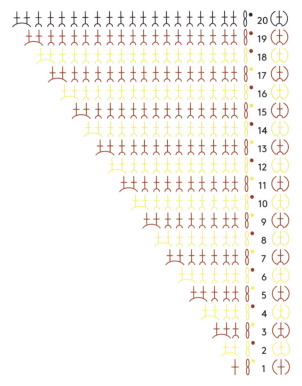

Round 20: 19 dc in back loop, 2 dc in the same st.
Round 19: 18 dc in back loop, 2 dc in the same st.
Round 18: 17 dc in back loop, 2 dc in the same st.
Round 17: 16 dc in back loop, 2 dc in the same st.
Round 16: 15 dc in back loop, 2 dc in the same st.
Round 15: 14 dc in back loop, 2 dc in the same st.
Round 14: 13 dc in back loop, 2 dc in the same st.
Round 13: 12 dc in back loop, 2 dc in the same st.
Round 12: 11 dc in back loop, 2 dc in the same st.
Round 11: 10 dc in back loop, 2 dc in the same st.
Round 10: 9 dc in back loop, 2 dc in the same st.
Round 9: 8 dc in back loop, 2 dc in the same st.
Round 8: 7 dc in back loop, 2 dc in the same st.
Round 7: 6 dc in back loop, 2 dc in the same st.
Round 6: 5 dc in back loop, 2 dc in the same st.
Round 5: 4 dc in back loop, 2 dc in the same st.
Round 4: 3 dc in back loop, 2 dc in the same st.
Round 3: 2 dc in back loop, 2 dc in the same st.
Round 2: 1 dc in back loop, 2 dc in the same st.
Round 1: 12 dc around magic ring (complete round).

The chart shows 1/6 of a round: repeat the chart 6 times per round after round 1. The symbol in brackets shows which stitch to crochet as a replacement for the two chain stitches of the turning chain when the chart is repeated. The text next to the chart specifies how many stitches are worked per sixth of a round.

Crochet with one colour at a time, leaving aside the colour you're not using, keeping it ready to pick up again in the next round. Finish all rounds by completing the final stitch in the colour you have been using. Crochet the slip stitch that marks the end of the round by yarning over with the next colour and pulling through the second chain stitch to finish the slip stitch. Your second colour is now on the hook. Turn the work and crochet the next round in the other direction. Make sure to place the previous round's yarn over the current yarn before you continue crocheting, as this will make the threads twist and the transition will become invisible.

### Assembly
Place the hexagons right sides facing together and sew back and forth in both hexagons' outer loops for an invisible join.

### Project suggestions
The hexagons are great for reversible projects, for example blankets, so that the effect of having different colours on each side stands out. A single hexagon can be made in a smaller size as a coaster, or enlarged to make a placemat.

GRANNY SQUARES 97

Here the even rounds' colours show.

Here the odd rounds' colours show.

# Fingal

*The Fingal, Trickster, Agaton, Daisy and Dainty hexagons are also based on the granny square. I have taken inspiration from the patterns seen in a kaleidoscope.*

**Level:** Intermediate
**Hexagon size:** 8 × 8cm
**Yarn:** 2-/3-ply cotton yarn
**Crochet hook:** 2.5mm or size needed to obtain tension
**Colours:** 2

The wrong side is just as nice as the right side since there aren't any 'floats' on the reverse because the colour changes are made in the treble crochet groups.

Start by making a magic ring for a closed centre or work 6 ch and sl st to first ch to form a ring.

Follow charts 1 and 2 on p. 100.

# Charts: Fingal (1–2)

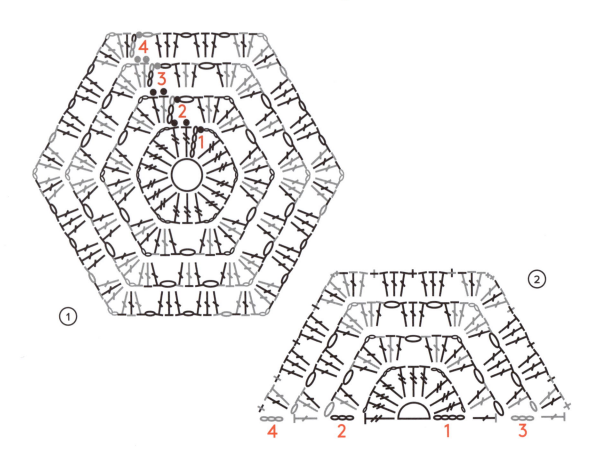

Chart 1 is a whole hexagon.

Chart 2 is a half hexagon. The half hexagon is worked back and forth in rows. It is neater if you twist the yarns at the edge so that the non-working yarn sits over the working one.

**Assembly**
Crochet the hexagons together as and when they're finished. This applies to whole and half hexagons.

Half hexagons are necessary if you need a completely straight edge for your project.

**Project suggestions using hexagons**
All hexagons are suitable for projects such as blankets and cushions. You only need whole hexagons if you want to assemble them into a whole cushion as, when folded, the edges slot together (front and back panels).

*7.5 × 7.5cm hexagon:* Trickster and Dainty. Child's blanket from 154 hexagons arranged 11 × 14 measures 82.5 × 105cm.

*8 × 8cm hexagon:* Fingal, Agaton and Daisy. Child's blanket from 154 hexagons arranged 11 × 14 measures 88 × 112cm.

# Trickster

*The Trickster hexagon is a variation of the Fingal where the pattern changes by varying the 2 colours in the treble crochet groups.*

---

**Level:** Easy, if you are used to colour changes
**Hexagon size:** 7.5 × 7.5cm
**Yarn:** 2-/3-ply cotton yarn
**Crochet hook:** 2.5mm or size needed to obtain tension
**Colours:** 2

---

The wrong side is just as nice as the right side since there aren't any 'floats' on the reverse because of the colour changes that are made in the treble crochet clusters.

Start by making a magic ring for a closed centre or work 6 ch and sl st to first ch to form a ring.

Follow charts 1 and 2 on p. 102.

# Charts: Trickster (1–2)

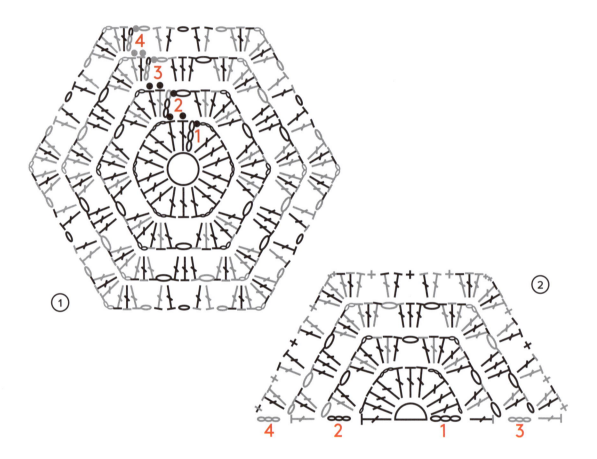

Chart 1 is a whole hexagon.

Chart 2 is a half hexagon, and the half hexagon is worked back and forth in rows.

When crocheting the half hexagon, it is neater if you twist the yarns at the edge so that the non-working yarn sits over the working one.

# Agaton

*The Agaton hexagon forms a kaleidoscopic pattern of simplified flowers.*

**Level:** Intermediate
**Hexagon size:** 8 × 8cm
**Yarn:** 2-/3-ply cotton yarn
**Crochet hook:** 2.5mm or size needed to obtain tension
**Colours:** 3

The wrong side is just as nice as the right side since there aren't any 'floats' on the reverse because the colour changes are made in the treble crochet groups.

Start by making a magic ring for a closed centre or work 6 ch and sl st to first ch to form a ring.

Follow charts 1 and 2 on p. 106.

# Charts: Agaton (1–2)

Chart 1 is a whole hexagon.

Chart 2 is a half hexagon. The half hexagon is worked back and forth in rows.

When crocheting the half hexagon, it is neater if you twist the yarns at the edge so that the non-working yarn sits over the working one.

Don't forget to cut the white yarn when you finish round 2 of the half hexagon. The colour comes back in round 4.

# Daisy

*The kaleidoscopic image in this hexagon forms a flowering meadow.*

---

**Level:** Intermediate. The tricky part is the assembly since the last round is made up of 3 colours. It requires concentration!

**Hexagon size:** 8 × 8cm

**Yarn:** 2-/3-ply cotton yarn

**Crochet hook:** 2.5mm or size needed to obtain tension

**Colours:** 4 colours per hexagon (vary the middle colour)

---

The wrong side is just as nice as the right side since there aren't any 'floats' on the reverse because the colour changes are made in the treble crochet groups.

Start by making a magic ring for a closed centre or work 6 ch and sl st to first ch to form a ring.

Follow charts 1 and 2 on p. 108.

## Charts: Daisy (1–2)

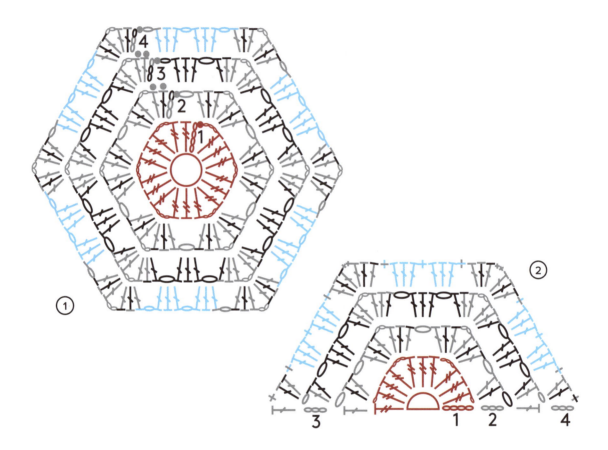

Chart 1 is a whole hexagon.

Cut the yarn once round 1 is finished since that colour won't come back in any other rounds.

Chart 2 is a half hexagon. The half hexagon is worked back and forth in rows, but make sure to crochet round 2 from the right side of the work. When crocheting the half hexagon, it is neater if you twist the yarns at the edge so that the non-working yarn sits over the working one.

### Assembly

Crochet the hexagons together as and when they're finished. The tricky part is crocheting the hexagons together neatly with others, since round 4 is worked with three colours.

# Dainty

*The Dainty hexagon has a kaleidoscopic effect looks woven.*

**Level:** Advanced
**Hexagon size:** 7.5 × 7.5cm
**Yarn:** 2-/3-ply cotton yarn
**Crochet hook:** 2.5mm or size needed to obtain tension
**Colours:** 2

The wrong side is just as nice as the right side since there aren't any 'floats' on the reverse because the colour changes are made in the treble crochet groups (1 black tr, 1 pink tr, 1 black tr).

Start by making a magic ring for a closed centre or work 6 ch and join to form a ring with 1 sl st.

Follow charts 1, 2 and 3 on p. 112. For this pattern you need two different half hexagons to make the pattern correct when assembling the hexagons.

## Charts: Dainty (1–3)

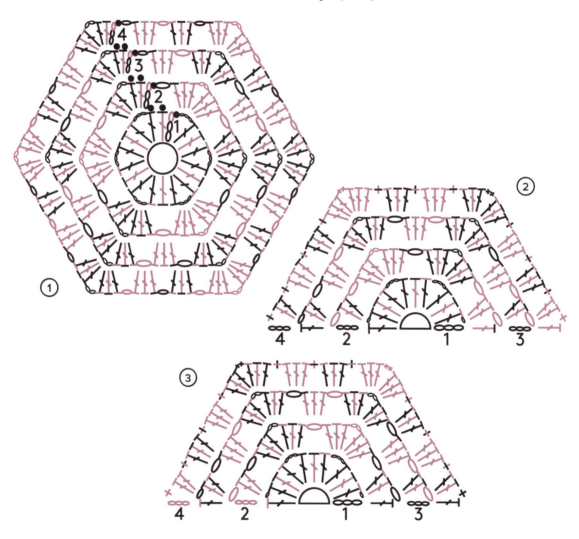

Chart 1 is a whole hexagon.

Chart 2 is a half hexagon.

Chart 3 is a half hexagon.

The half hexagons are worked back and forth in rows. When crocheting a half hexagon, it is neater if you twist the yarns at the edge so that the non-working yarn sits over the working one.

**Assembly**

Crochet the hexagons together as and when they're finished.

The half hexagons in charts 2 and 3 are mirrored to make the pattern correct when you assemble them together with the whole hexagons. For both hexagons the following apply: when crocheting a half hexagon together with a whole hexagon, crochet black/pink/black corner ch sp with the opposite hexagon's black/pink/black ch sp. At the all pink ch sp, crochet it together with the opposite hexagon's all pink ch sp.

Right side.

Wrong side.

# MOSAIC CROCHET

Mosaic crochet is a simple technique as you crochet with one colour per round, and the colour you aren't currently using you set aside at the beginning/end of the round. The square is always crocheted from the right side of the work and worked in the round. The wrong side turns stripy!

The stitches used are chain stitches, slip stitches, double crochet in the back loop and long treble crochet.

The long treble crochet stitches sit on top of the work and are inserted 2 rounds down. Work the long treble crochet by yarning over and inserting the hook into the front loop 2 rounds further down – beige long treble crochet is worked into a beige front loop and black long treble crochet in a black front loop. Then continue with double crochet in the back loop.

All rounds start with 2 ch (which counts as the round's first dc) and are finished with 1 sl st in the second ch st. Then insert the hook into the next stitch's back loop and yarn over with the new colour, pulling through.

# How to read crochet charts

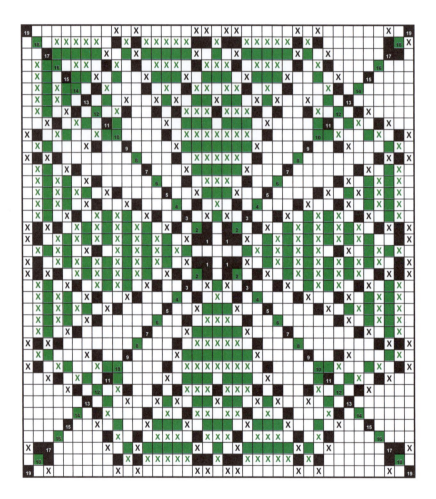

The chart shows which stitches you should crochet each round and when to make colour changes. The numbers specify which round it is. In the key to symbols on page 117, the symbols for the stitches you should crochet are explained.

# Key to symbols

**Filled squares with numbers** in each corner ch sp specifies which colour you should use for the round and which round you are on. Work 1 dc, 2 ch, 1 dc in each corner ch sp.

**Filled squares without numbers** show where to insert the hook for long treble crochet – it should not be worked in this round. Instead it should be worked in the round where the square with an X is.

**Empty squares** mean that you should work dc in the back loop only of the stitch in the previous row.

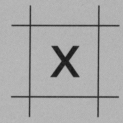

**Squares with an X** show where you should work a long treble crochet. The hook is inserted 2 rounds down in the front loop (marked with a filled square without a number).

On the following pages are two large mosaic crochet patterns: Stella, and William Morris. Don't get intimidated by the charts, which might look complicated at first. Just follow them round by round. When you have crocheted one side of a square it can be a good idea to rotate the chart 90 degrees to be able to follow it more easily.

# Stella

*I discovered mosaic crochet in the spring of 2007, and this star was the first one I crocheted. The pattern is inspired by folk stars that can be found in textile culture all around the world. Beige and black give the feeling of blackwork embroidery.*

**Level:** Fairly easy

**Large square:** 11 × 11cm (one square is made up of 1284 stitches)

**Small square:** 5.5 × 5.5cm

**Yarn:** 2-/3-ply cotton yarn

**Crochet hook:** 2.5mm or size needed to obtain tension

**Colours:** 2 main colours (beige and black), red and pink for the middle of the stars, red for the border

**Long treble crochet:** yarn over and insert the hook into the front loop 2 rounds down – beige long treble crochet is worked in a beige front loop and black long treble crochet is worked in the black front loop. Finish the treble crochet as normal. When it's finished it will sit on top of the work.

Start by making a magic ring for a closed centre or work 6 ch and sl st to first ch to form a ring.

Round 1: Working around the magic ring, *3 dc, 2 ch* and repeat from * to * 4 times in total. Finish the round with 1 sl st in the first dc.

Start all rounds with 2 ch which form the first stitch of the round.

Finish all rounds with 1 sl st in the second ch st. Then insert the hook into the next stitch's back loop and make a yarn over with the new colour and pull through.

It's easier to follow the charts (see pp. 128–145) if you turn the book 90 degrees when you have finished one side of the round.

# Project: Stella Cushion 1

*This square cushion is made up of large and small squares. You can, of course, make a rectangular cushion too.*

---

**Cushion measurements:** 55 × 55cm

**You will need:** 24 large squares and 4 small squares for the front panel

**Charts:** 1–5, 6a

---

### Method

Sew the squares together as you go, working from the wrong side in the back loops with the same black cotton yarn that you used for the squares. On the right side, the front loops will form a decorative edge.

Crochet 4 small squares following chart 6a on p. 133 (black) and assemble. Crochet a red border around them.

**Red border:** Dc in the back loops. In the corner ch sps work 1 dc, 2 ch, 1 dc. Between 2 squares crochet 3 spike dcs which sit on top of the work: 1 dc in one square's corner ch sp, 1 dc between the two squares inserted in round 6, 1 dc in the next square's corner ch sp.

Crochet 4 squares following chart 1, 4 squares following chart 2 (black) on pp. 128–129, and assemble with the small squares. Careful with star placement: the squares have corners that form different patterns when you put them together. Refer to the picture on page 120. Crochet a red border around everything as before. Here the longest spike stitch is worked by inserting the hook into round 15. Crochet 8 squares following chart 3, 4 squares following chart 4, and 4 squares following chart 5 (beige) and sew together with rest (see pp. 130–132).

Crochet a red border around the whole work. Dc in the back loops. Between the squares work 1 dc in the corner ch sp, 1 dc between the squares with insertion of the hook in round 15, 1 dc in the next corner ch sp. In the four outer corner ch sps, work 1 dc, 1 ch, 1 dc.

Now you have a front panel: sew it to a back panel made from a sturdier fabric like linen or cotton. You can fill the cushion with stuffing or use a cushion insert. Decorate the corners with pompoms (p. 40) or tassels, if you wish.

---

*For the Stella Cushion 1 you will need*

| Charts | Number of squares |
|---|---|
| 1 | 4 |
| 2 | 4 |
| 3 | 8 |
| 4 | 4 |
| 5 | 4 |
| 6a | 4 |

# Project: Stella Cushion 2

**Cushion measurements:** 55 × 55cm

**You will need:** 12 large squares and 52 small squares for the front panel

**Charts:** 6a, 6b, 6c and 7

### Method
Sew the squares together as you finish them, working from the wrong side in the back loops with the same black cotton yarn that you used for the squares. On the right side, the front loops on both squares will form a decorative edge.

Crochet 16 small squares following chart 6a on p. 133 (black) and assemble.

Crochet a red border around the assembled small squares.

**Red border:** double crochet in the back loops. In the corner ch sps, work 1 dc, 2 ch, 1 dc. Between 2 squares, crochet 3 spike dcs which sit on top of the work: 1 dc in one square's corner ch sp, 1 dc between the two squares inserted in round 6 and 1 dc in the next square's corner ch sp.

Crochet 12 large squares following chart 7 (8 black and 4 beige stars; the chart shows a beige star and you get the black one by swapping the colours) on p. 134. Assemble with the first squares. Be careful with the stars: the squares have different corners that form different patterns when you put them together. Refer to the picture on the previous page.

Crochet a red border around everything as before. Here the longest spike stitch is worked by inserting the hook into round 15.

*For the Stella Cushion 2 you will need*

| Charts | Number of squares |
|---|---|
| 6a | 32 |
| 6b | 16 |
| 6c | 4 |
| black 7 | 8 |
| beige 7 | 4 |

Crochet 36 small squares following charts 6a, 6b and 6c (16 black, 16 beige and 4 red) on p. 133 and assemble with the rest.

Crochet a black and red border around the whole work with dc in the back loops. In the corner ch sps, work 1 dc, 2 ch, 1 dc. Crochet with black yarn around the red and beige squares, and with red yarn along the black squares.

Now you have a front panel for the cushion. Sew it together with a back panel from a thicker fabric like linen or cotton. You can fill the cushion with stuffing or use a cushion insert. Decorate the corners with pompoms (see p. 40) or tassels, if you wish.

# Project: Stella Blanket

*This large blanket is an advanced project, not because the squares themselves are difficult to crochet, but because of the time it will take to crochet and assemble all the squares. Sometimes the star has 3 colours, but you still only crochet with one colour per round.*

## Blanket measurements: 145 × 178cm
## You will need: 154 large squares
## Charts: 8–20

The blanket is made up of 154 squares and each square is made of 1284 stitches. That is 197736 stitches in total for the squares (and I haven't counted in the borders). I have crocheted the squares in cotton yarn, but you can also crochet in wool yarn. The pattern might look slightly less distinctive in wool.

For crochet squares follow charts 8–18 (see pp. 135–145) and for borders follow charts 19–20 (see p. 145).

For charts 11–14 (see pp. 138–141) I have been experimenting with and swapping the colours; the red for pink, orange or dark red and so on.

### Method
Crochet the squares for the inner section following charts 10–15, and assemble. Be careful with the stars: the squares have different corners that form different patterns when you put them together. Refer to the picture on the previous page.

Crochet a border around the assembled squares in crab stitch (see right).

*For the Stella Blanket you will need*

| Charts | Number of squares |
| --- | --- |
| 8 | 42 |
| 9 | 4 |
| 10 | 15 |
| 11 | 10 |
| 12 | 25 |
| 13 | 5 |
| 14 | 5 |
| 15 | 10 |
| 16 | 28 |
| 17 | 6 |
| 18 | 4 |

**Crab stitch border:** this is worked from the right side of the work. They are worked as dc but backwards, left to right. Insert the hook into the back loop and work a dc. It's better to use a thicker hook so that the stitches don't get too compact. In corner ch sps, work 1 dc, 2 ch, 1 dc.

Next, crochet the squares for the inner border following charts 9, 16 and 17 (see pp. 136, 143, 144) and assemble with the first squares.

Crochet a border following chart 19 (see p. 145) around everything. In the corner ch sp always work 1 dc, 2 ch, 1 dc.

Crochet the squares for the outer border following charts 8 and 18 (see pp. 135 and 145). Assemble with the earlier squares with an embroidered border. Note that round 18 in chart 18 is worked in beige crab stitches: dc backwards from left to right from the right side of the work (see below).

**Embroidered border:** with black yarn dc in the back loops for 5 rounds around the whole work. Thread a darning needle with beige yarn and sew a zigzag pattern in the front loops.

Crochet a border according to chart 20 (see p. 145) around the whole work.

» Stars, particularly the eight-pointed star, the octagon, the rose, are recurrent in all periods and in the textile art of all countries. No matter how we fret and toil, we pattern designers will hardly be able to surpass this handful of useful geometric shapes, already repeated in their thousands. «

*– Märta Måås-Fjetterström (1873–1941)*

## Charts: Stella (1–2)

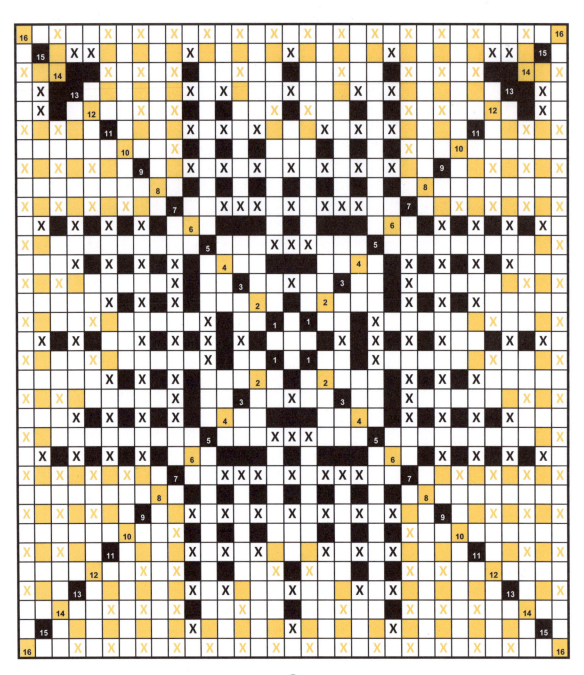

①

②

## Charts: Stella (3–4)

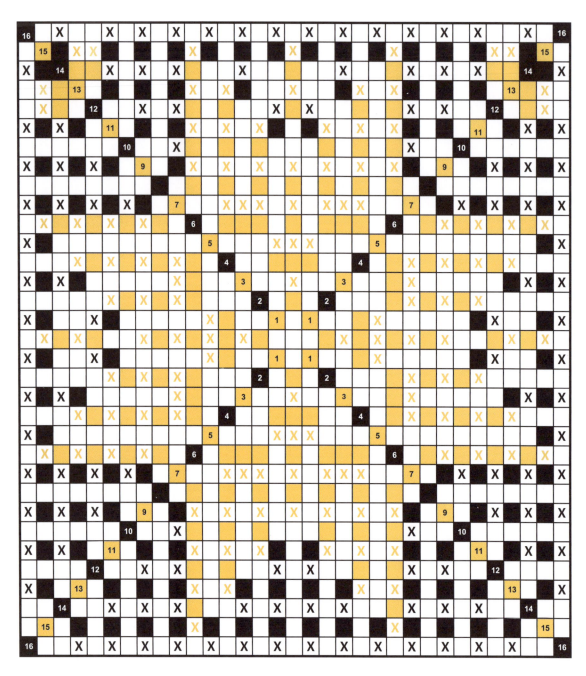

③

MOSAIC CROCHET

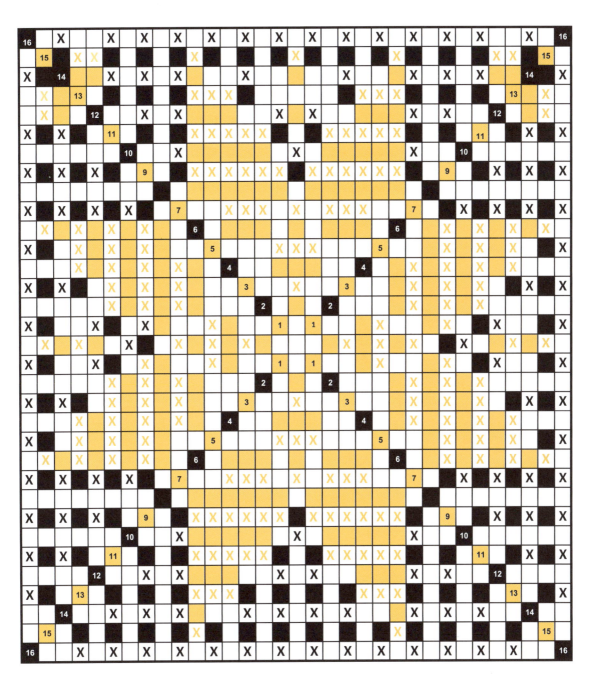

(4)

## Charts: Stella (5–6)

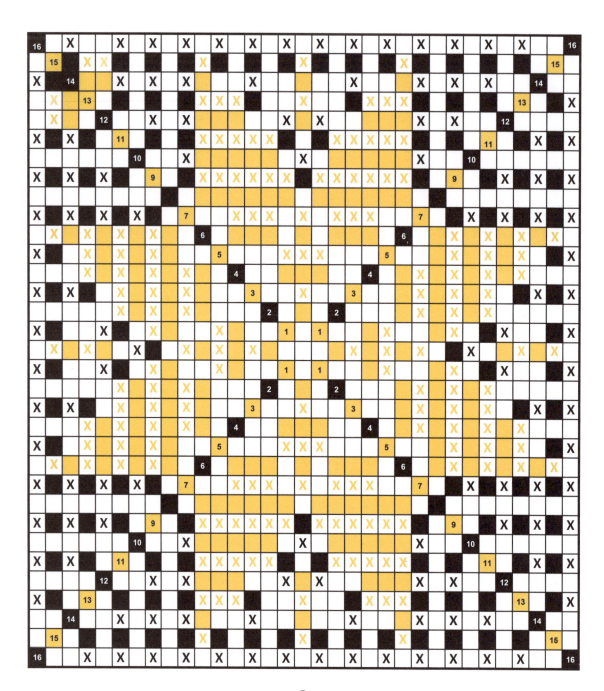

⑤

MOSAIC CROCHET

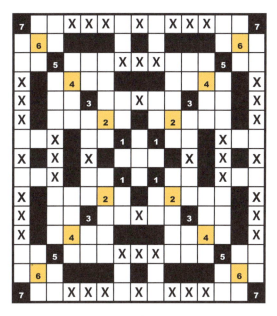

(6a)

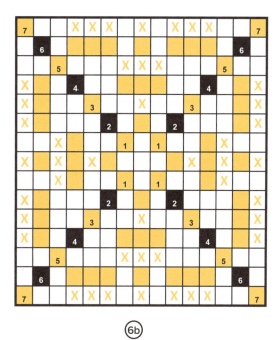

(6b)

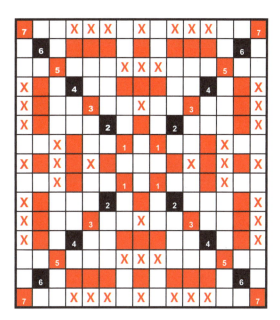

(6c)

## Charts: Stella (7–8)

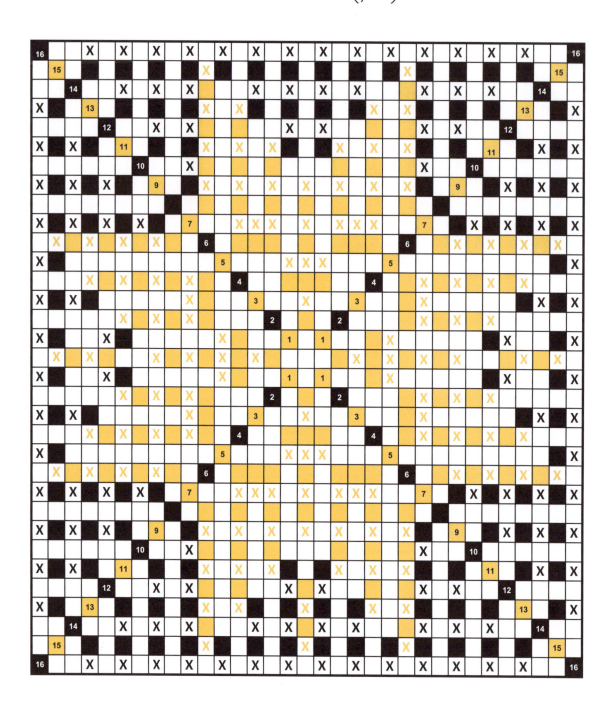

⑧

## Charts: Stella (9–10)

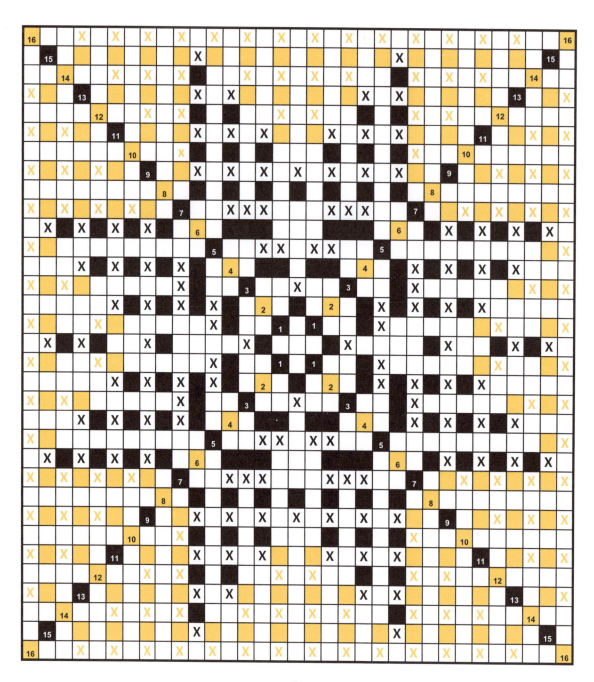

(9)

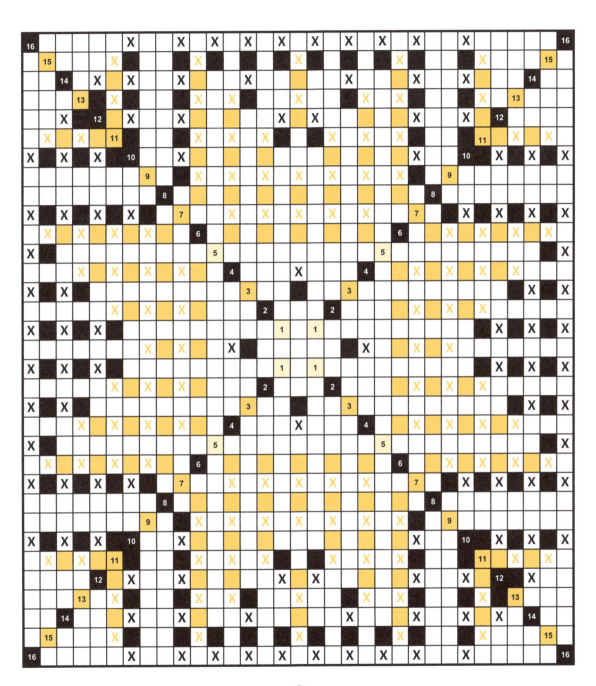

# Charts: Stella (11–12)

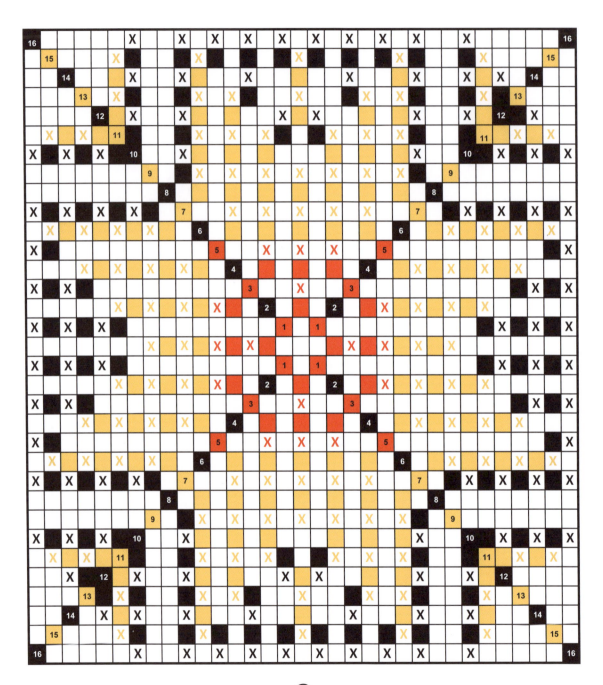

(11)

MOSAIC CROCHET

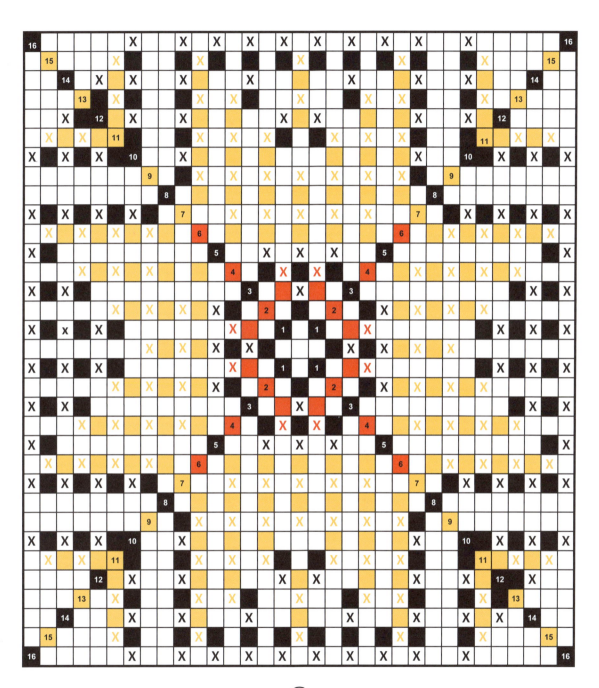

12

## **Charts:** Stella (13–14)

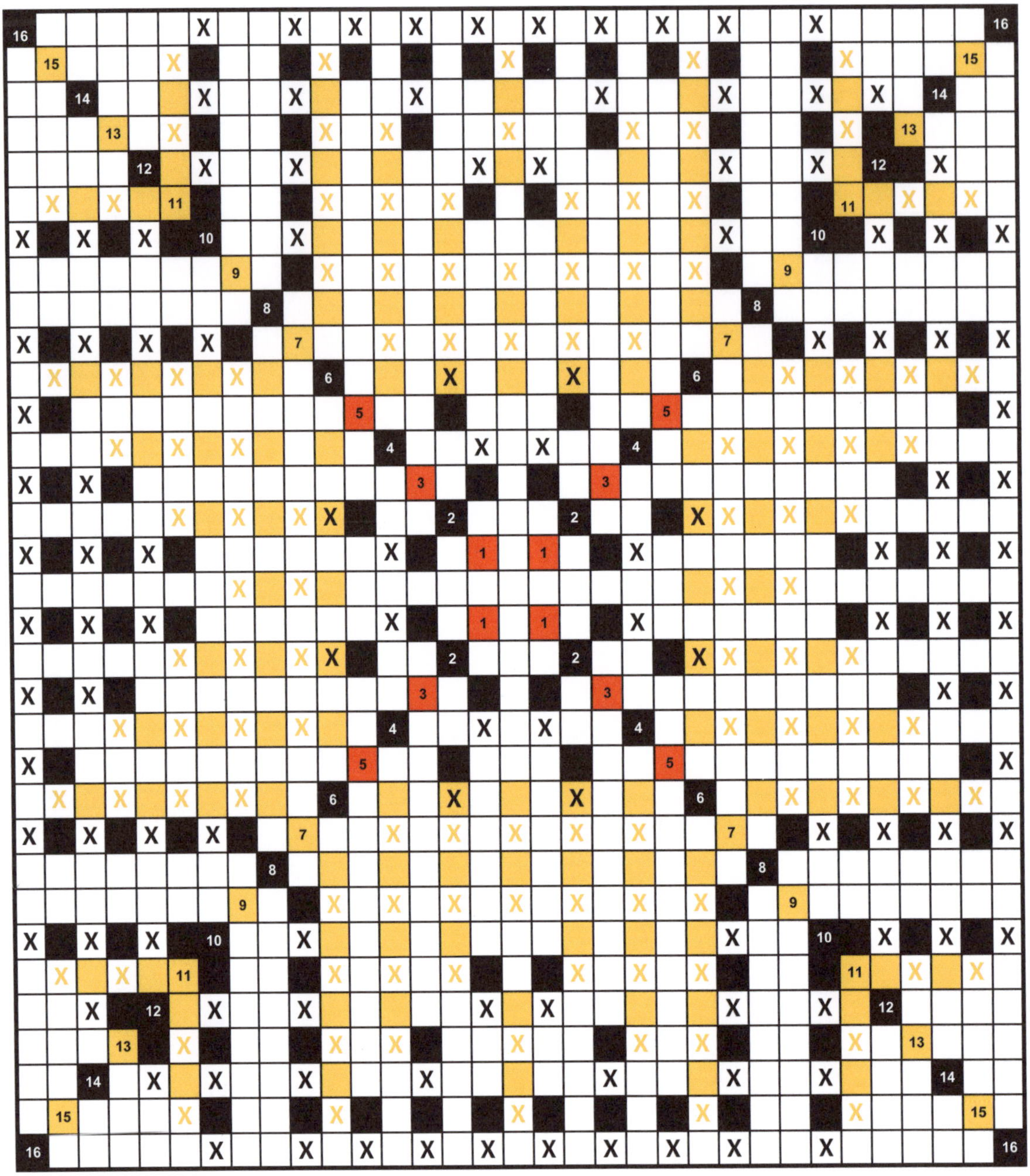

13

# MOSAIC CROCHET

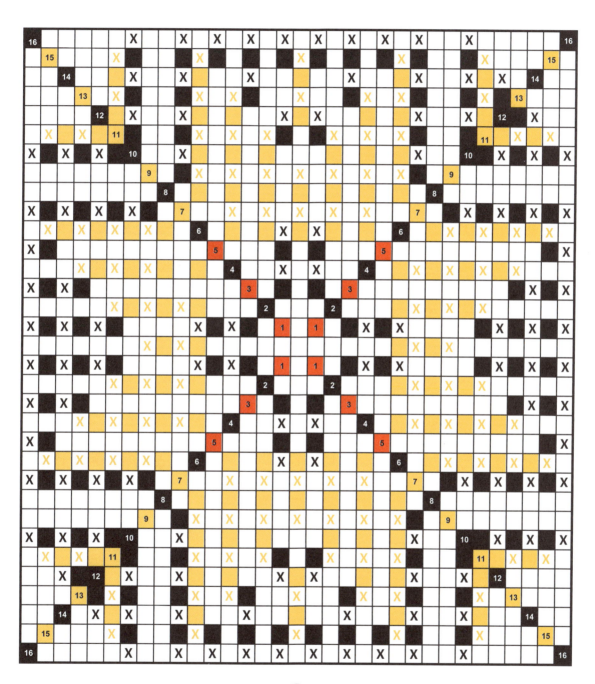

(14)

## Charts: Stella (15–16)

⑮

# MOSAIC CROCHET

## Charts: Stella (17–20)

(17)

MOSAIC CROCHET 145

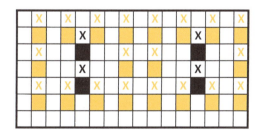

# William Morris

*I was inspired by the luscious patterns that William Morris (1834–1896) created when designing these squares. He was a British artist, designer, textile designer and writer, and was a prominent figure within the Arts and Crafts movement. His patterns for textiles, tapestries, carpets, wallpaper and tiles transformed Victorian interiors. He was an advocate for the importance of handicrafts and used natural forms in his designs.*

**Level:** Fairly easy even if the charts might look complicated at first
**Large square:** 13 × 13cm (one square is 1752 stitches: one pattern repetition is 4 squares)
**Small square:** 7 × 7cm
**Yarn:** 2–/3–ply cotton yarn
**Crochet hook:** 2.5mm or size needed to obtain tension

## Method

The details of which charts to follow for the two William Morris style projects are given with the projects. The squares for both are worked as given here.

**Long treble crochet:** yarn over and insert the hook into the front loop 2 rounds below – green long treble crochet is worked in the green front loops and black long treble crochet is worked in the black front loosp. Finish the treble crochet as normal. The finished long treble crochet will sit on top of the work.

Start by making a magic ring for a closed centre or work 6 ch and sl st to first ch to form a ring.

Round 1: Working around the ring, *3 dc, 2 ch* and repeat from * to * 4 times in total. Finish the round with 1 sl st in the first dc. Start all rounds with a 2 ch turning chain which counts as the first stitch on the round.

Finish all rounds with 1 sl st in the second ch st. Then insert the hook into the next stitch's back loop and yarn over with the new colour, then pull through.

Crochet the square in the round and to read the chart correctly it is a good idea to rotate the book 90 degrees after each finished side.

If you look carefully, you can see a black and green flower with four 'petals' in the middle of the assembled squares. It's inspired by the flower of the starfish plant (Orbea variegata), a small, 10cm high, succulent without leaves from South Africa. In Sweden we grow it as a houseplant.

## Assembly

Sew the squares together as and when they're finished from the wrong side in the back loops with the black yarn. On the right side the front loops will form a decorative edge.

Large square. 4 squares together will form a repeat pattern.

MOSAIC CROCHET 149

Small square. You can choose whether to crochet a small flower in the corners (chart 6, p. 159) or not (chart 7, p. 159).

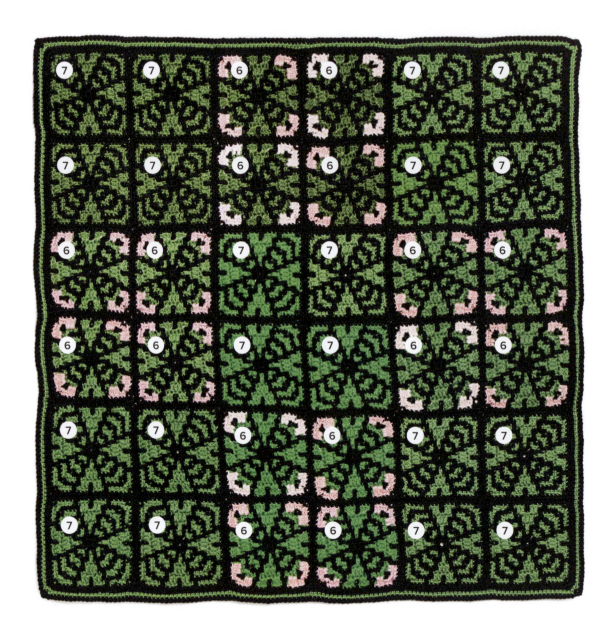

# Project: William Morris Cushion

*The small square is a variation of the first 9 rounds of the large square. One repeat pattern section is made up of 4 squares which form a pattern with both leaves and circles. Here I have made a cushion. By crocheting flowers in a contrasting colour in some of the corners, the colours in the cushion will pop.*

**Cushion measurement:** 44 × 44cm
**You will need:** 36 small squares for the front panel
**Charts:** 6 and 7

### Method
*Chart 6:* (p. 159) this square has small flowers in a contrasting colour in each corner of round 8. The yarn for the flower is only used in the corners. Cut the yarn when the stitches in each corner are finished. The remaining stitches in round 8 are worked in green. Crochet around the green yarn when working the flower corner stitches.

Join 4 identical squares into blocks (chart 6 or chart 7, p. 159) then join the blocks together.

Crochet a border around the finished panel.

### Border
Dc in the back loop from the right side of the work. In the corner ch sps work: 1 dc, 2 ch, 1 dc. I have crocheted one round in black, one in green and finished with a last round in black.

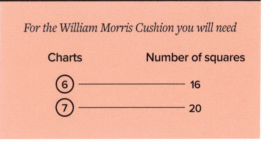

*For the William Morris Cushion you will need*

| Charts | Number of squares |
|---|---|
| 6 | 16 |
| 7 | 20 |

Now you have a front panel for the cushion. Sew it together with a back panel made from a sturdy fabric like linen or cotton. You can also crochet another panel the same way and use that for the cushion back, and the cushion can be turned either way. You can choose whether to fill the cushion with stuffing or use a cushion insert.

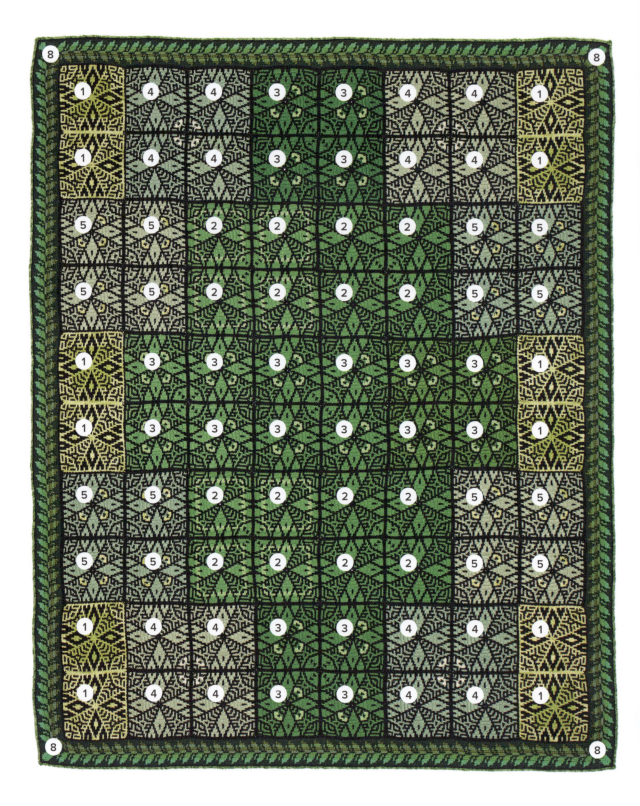

# Project: William Morris Blanket

*In this blanket the colours in the squares vary, and the primary colour and the background colour change place. The pattern will still be clear, and the surface will come to life.*

**Blanket measurements:** 117 × 143cm
**You will need:** 80 large squares
**Charts:** 1–5 and 8

### Method

*Chart 4:* (p. 157) one of the corners is worked in a contrasting colour in round 16. The yarn for the corner is only used there. Cut the yarn when the corner stitches are finished. The rest of the round is worked in black, and the black yarn is crocheted around when working the coloured corner.

*Chart 5:* (p. 158) this square has small flowers in contrasting colour in each of round 8. The yarn for the flowers is only used in the corners. Cut the yarn when the stitches in each corner are finished. The remaining stitches in round 8 are worked in green. Crochet in and around the green yarn when working the flower corner stitches.

One repeat pattern section is made up of 4 squares.

*For the William Morris Blanket you will need*

| Charts | Number of squares |
|---|---|
| 1 | 12 |
| 2 | 16 |
| 3 | 20 |
| 4 | 16 |
| 5 | 16 |

Crochet the squares for the central area following charts 2, 3, 4 and 5 (pp. 155–158) and assemble in groups of 4 arranged 2 x 2. Then assemble the groups of 4 with each other.

Crochet 12 squares following chart 1. Join these into pairs, and then join the pairs.

Crochet the border according to chart 8 (p. 159) around the whole work.

**Border:** the border is worked in multiple colours and is worked from the right side with double crochet in the back loops. In the corner ch sps work 1 dc, 2 ch, 1 dc. I have used different shades of green for each round.

## Charts: William Morris (1–2)

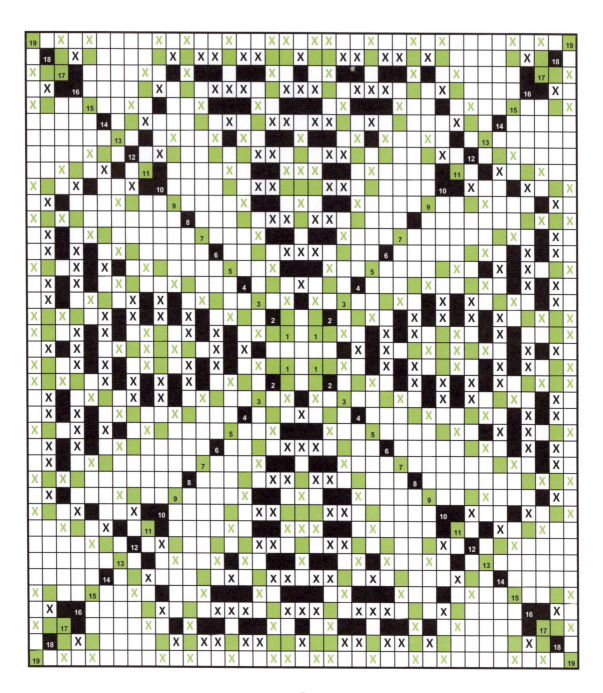

①

# MOSAIC CROCHET

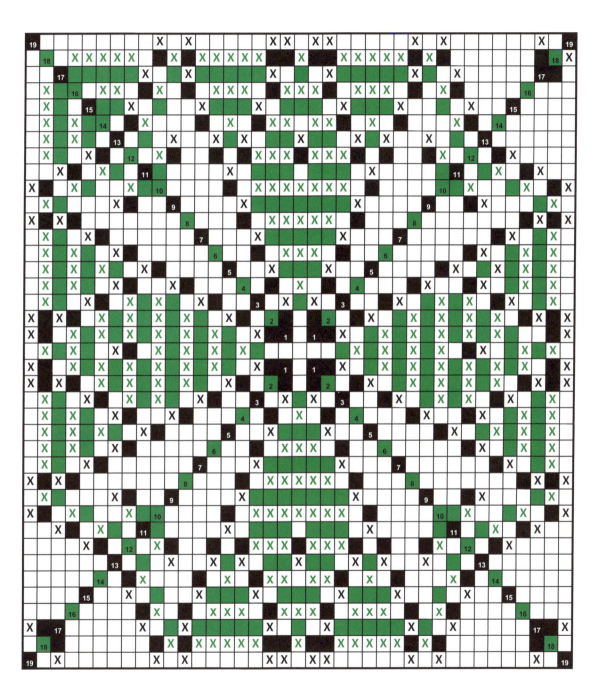

(2)

## Charts: William Morris (3–4)

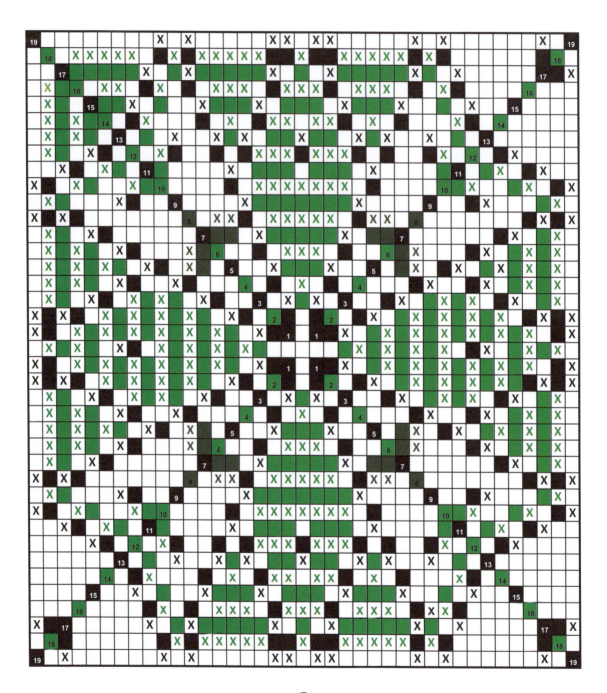

③

MOSAIC CROCHET 157

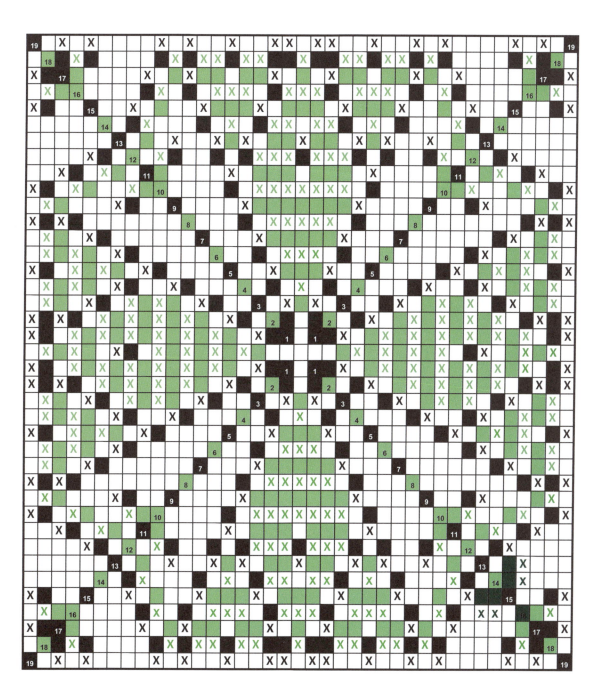

## Charts: William Morris (5–8)

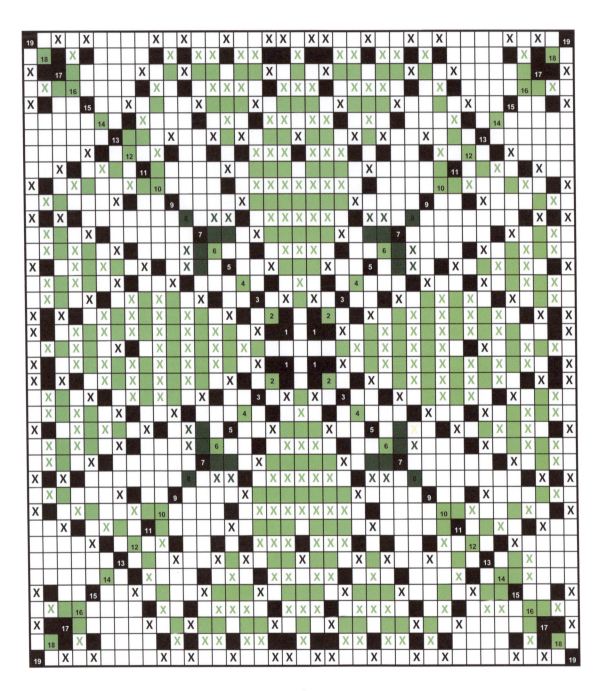

MOSAIC CROCHET

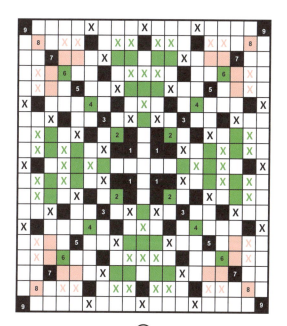

(6)

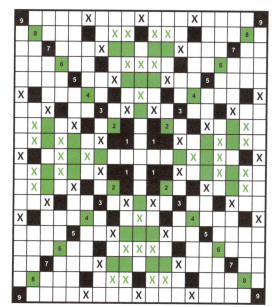

(7)

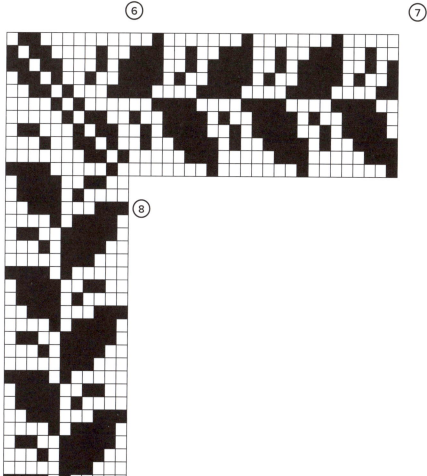

(8)

# Basic patterns for clothes

Here are a few basic patterns that you can use if you want to turn your squares into clothes. I have made the patterns to work with the size of my squares, but the size of the garment will, of course, depend on how large your squares are. Take your own measurements, measure your squares and see how the jigsaw puzzle will fit together. See the patterns as a base that you can adjust as needed.

## Vest

The chart for the vest is based on squares that measure 5.5 × 5.5cm

**Squares in the book that measure 5.5 × 5.5cm**
Jambo, Agda and Hilda

| Vest measurement | |
|---|---|
| Width | 60.5cm |
| Length | approx. 74cm |
| Shoulder strap | 33cm long |
| Cuff width | approx. 30cm |

**Total number of squares:** 223 whole squares (the 4 half squares by each armhole are 2 whole squares that have been folded in half)

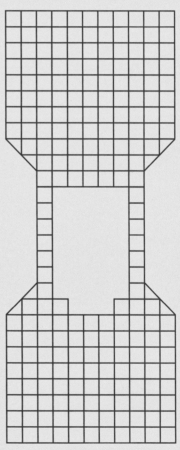

# Ladies' jumper

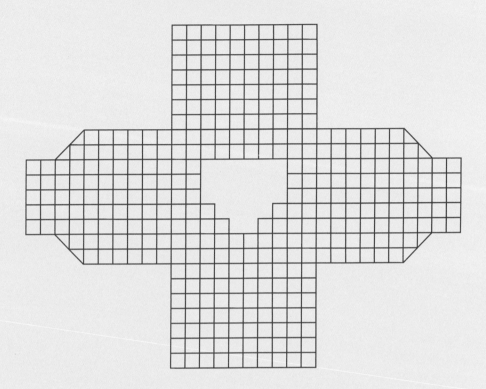

The chart for the ladies' jumper is based on squares that measure 5.5 × 5.5cm

**Squares in the book that measure 5.5 × 5.5cm**
Jambo, Agda and Hilda

| Ladies' jumper measurements | |
|---|---|
| Width | 55cm |
| Length | approx. 63cm |
| Sleeve width | approx. 25cm at the armhole, approx. 14cm at the cuff |
| Sleeve length | 55cm |

**Total number of squares:** 362 whole squares (the half squares by each cuff are whole squares that have been folded in half at the sleeve)

If you want to make a jacket or a cardigan instead of a jumper, don't crochet together the squares at the centre front. Sew in a zip or make button bands for buttons. Crochet a button band with either 3 dc in each ch sp and 1 ch in between or 3 treble crochet in each ch sp and 1 ch in between. See also the long cardigan on p. 162 for instructions for button bands.

To make the crocheted pattern shine, front and back panels can be assembled with patterned squares while the sleeves can be one colour. Patterned squares can become a nice cuff finish on the sleeve.

# Long cardigan

The chart for the long cardigan is based on squares that measure 10 × 10cm

**Squares in the book that measure 10 × 10cm**
Acke and Svea

| Long cardigan measurements | |
|---|---|
| Width | 60cm |
| Length | approx. 135cm |
| Sleeve width | approx. 35cm at the armhole, approx. 15cm at the cuff |
| Sleeve length | 60cm |

**Total number of squares:** 216 whole squares (the 8 half squares in the chart are 4 whole squares that have been folded in half)

**Button bands**
*The band with buttons*: dc along the front edge (1 dc in each stitch and 1 dc in the ch sp). Work a couple of rows to required width

*The band with buttonholes*: work like the other edge, but where you want the buttonholes work 2 ch (measure the buttons you want to use, and ch more if needed so that they can go through the buttonhole) and skip 2 stitches. Continue with dc between the buttonholes ch sts. In the next row work 2 dc in the buttonhole ch sps, and you've got your buttonholes.

---

# Shawl

The chart for the shawl is based on squares that measure 12 × 12cm.

**Squares in the book that measure 12 × 12cm**
Dialogue, Delight and Xara.

| Shawl measurements | |
|---|---|
| Width | 156cm |
| Height | 84cm |

**Total number of squares:** 49

# Waistcoat or slipover

The chart for this waistcoat or slipover is based on squares that measure 5.5 × 5.5cm or 6.5 × 6.5cm. The smaller squares makes a smaller garment and the larger squares a larger garment.

The chart shows a waistcoat with either buttons or a zip at the front. See instructions for button bands opposite on p. 162.

**Squares in the book that measure 5.5 × 5.5cm**
Jambo, Agda and Hilda

| Waistcoat measurements 5.5 × 5.5cm | |
| --- | --- |
| Width | 55cm |
| Length | approx. 58cm |
| Armhole width | approx. 25cm |

**Total number of squares:** 178

**Squares in the book that measure 6.5 × 6.5cm**
Aida and Zola

| Waistcoat measurements (6.5cm square) | |
| --- | --- |
| Width | 65cm |
| Length | approx. 68cm |
| Armhole width | approx. 29cm |

**Total number of squares:** 178

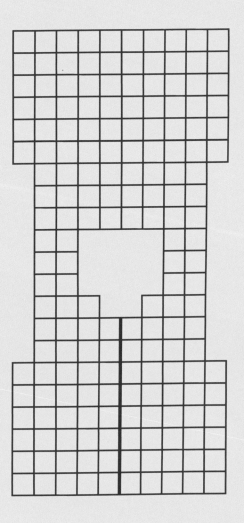

# Assembly

You can sew or crochet your squares together. For the best results, block your project (see p. 166).

### Securing yarn ends
When you have finished your squares, cut the yarn, pull the yarn end through the final stitch with the hook and pull it tight. Secure the yarn ends by knotting them and then sewing them up and down in adjacent stitches on the wrong side of the work for a few centimetres. Try to secure into stitches that are the same colour.

### Sewing squares together
*Sew in the back loop:* I usually sew squares together by placing them with right sides facing up and sewing them together in the back loops of each square, working back and forth (not with whip stitches).

*Whip stitches with colour effect:* the photograph opposite shows single coloured granny squares that I have sewn together using whip stitches in other colours to get an edging around the squares. Sew from the right side with 4–5 whip stitches in each chain space.

### Crocheting squares together
*Crocheting squares together as and when they're finished:* I assemble a lot of the squares, particularly granny squares, by crocheting them together in the last round. This creates a nice transition in the pattern and the round crocheted to assemble the squares won't disrupt the pattern design. Several of the patterns are made up of multiple squares (usually 4) that form a repeat pattern.

This is how to crochet the squares together (see illustrations opposite). Crochet square 1, crochet square 2, and when you come to the final round, work square 2 together with square 1. Start at the top right corner in the ch sp on square 2 and at the bottom right corner ch sp on square 1. Work 3 tr, 1 ch in square 2 and then 1 dc in the ch sp on square 1. Continue with 3 tr in the corner ch sp on square 2 and then 1 dc in the ch sp on square 1. Continue the same way along the side that the squares share.

Crochet square 3 and on the last round crochet together with square 1, referring to illustration opposite.

Crochet square 4 and on the last round crochet together with square 2 and square 3. When you come to the point where all squares meet in the corners, first work 3 tr in the corner ch sp on square 4, then 1 dc in the corner ch sp on square 3 and 1 dc in the corner ch sp on square 2 and 3 tr in the corner ch sp on square 4.

*Crocheting finished squares together:* if you want to crochet together finished squares later, place the squares right sides facing and crochet together with slip stitches or double crochet in either one or the other of the edge stitches' loops (front or back). It's a slightly bulkier assembly than when you crochet the squares together in the final round.

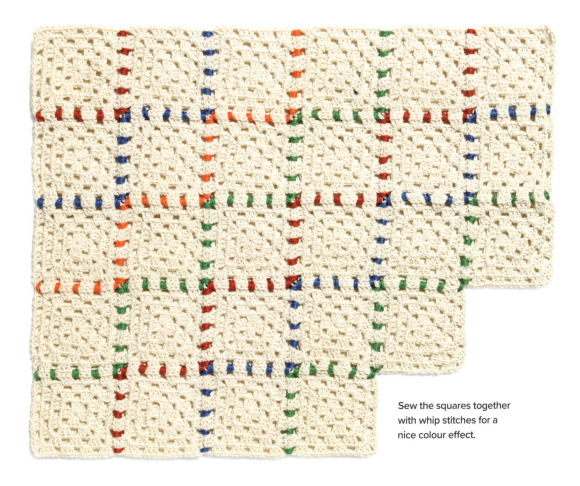

Sew the squares together with whip stitches for a nice colour effect.

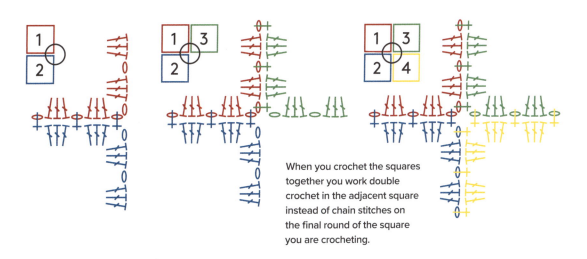

When you crochet the squares together you work double crochet in the adjacent square instead of chain stitches on the final round of the square you are crocheting.

### Crocheting and sewing squares together

Crochet the squares together as you work in each corner ch sp respectively. Thereafter sew the squares together with each other from the wrong side of the work with stitches back and forth in the back loops of each square. With this technique, the work will be just as nice on the wrong side!

### Mixing different patterns in one project

Who said that a project should be made up of squares with only one pattern? Or the same sized patterns? Try to assemble a square panel with squares in one pattern and combine it with a square panel with squares in a different, perhaps similar, pattern.

### Crocheted border

If you want to get a nice finish on a project, you can crochet a border around the squares after you've sewn or crocheted them together. There are a few borders in this book that you can use (see pp. 26, 32, 76, 121, 123, 125, 126, 145 and 159).

A standard border for granny squares is to work 3 tr in each ch sp with 1 ch in between. When 2 squares meet, work 3 tr in the final corner ch sp, 1 ch, 3 tr in the next square's corner ch sp. In the project's corner ch sp, work 3 tr, 2 ch, 3 tr.

The border can also be made up of several rounds of double crochet, preferably worked in the back loops for a flexible edge. If you want a sturdier border, crochet through both loops. If you're making a border around a square project, work 1 dc, 2 ch, 1 dc in the corner ch sps to get a 'sharp' corner.

### Blocking

The squares can get a bit wonky on the edges since your tension can vary from time to time. If you crochet with different yarn qualities that can also affect the shape of the square. Blocking the squares is then necessary to make sure the result is as good as possible. This means that you stretch the finished project to desired shape by spraying it with water and fix it in place with dressmaker's pins to a suitable surface. Then leave it to air dry.

Larger works I usually block as I go along. Blocking larger projects requires a bit of space. I use a standard children's jigsaw-puzzle mat that I put together depending on what size I need – it's both simple and cheap. A sleeping mat will also do the job. It's important that you can insert pins into the surface. Standard dressmaker's pins will work fine for stretching out the project.

When I need to block multiples of a square, I usually use a thicker styrofoam board. I spray the first square with water, place it on the board and insert standard double-pointed knitting needles in the corners of the square. Then I add on more squares on top and spray each one, perhaps 5 in each pile.

### Ironing

Ironing a project into shape can sometimes be an alternative to blocking it. Make sure, however, not to iron the work directly. Instead, either use a damp pressing cloth or the steam function on your iron. If the iron doesn't steam properly you can dampen the project with a spray bottle at the same time.

# Colours

When I was little, my favourite colour was yellow. Everything had to be yellow, from the squash I drank to the wallpaper in my room which had yellow roses. Today I don't have a particular favourite colour, but when I think about new structures and patterns I automatically think in black, white and shades of grey with red as an accent colour.

Personally, I think it's quite tricky to combine colours properly – a few colours are easy but more makes it harder. The colours you choose for a new project can at first sight look amazing, but as you work you notice that some colours seem to get dulled down by their surrounding friends, or become too dominant, and it doesn't look as you imagined at all. A simple tip to see if the chosen colours have the right contrast is to photograph the yarns with your mobile phone and change the picture to black and white. The colours that are too close to each other might have to be swapped out – unless a barely noticeable contrast is what you're after for your pattern.

**Simple tips for matching colours**

1. Go with your gut feeling and dare to try different and unexpected combinations of colours that you normally wouldn't choose.

2. Remember that no colour combinations are right or wrong.

3. An accent colour always brightens things up a bit!

4. There are free apps you can download for your phone that can convert an image to chosen colours. One app that I use is Adobe Capture.

5. Complementary colours are good to use if you want to highlight certain details in a pattern. Complementary colours are the two colours that are the furthest away and opposite each other in the colour wheel and are the colours that highlight and enhance each other the most. For example red and green, yellow and purple, blue and orange.

6. Choose three colours that sit close to each other colourwise: for example yellow, orange and red. You get the best result if they are mixed according to the 60–30–10 rule. This means that the main colour gets 60 percent of the colour scheme. The second colour is a complement and is 30 percent. The third colour works as an accent colour at 10 percent.

7. Several hues of one colour creates an elegant expression.

8. By using warm colours (red, orange, yellow) and cool colours (blue, purple, green) you can create different surfaces. The warm colours can make a surface seem smaller in size while the cool can make it seem larger.

# Creativity and inspiration

I have been fascinated by patterns, structures and colours for as long as I can remember. When I was little I loved drawing and cutting out pictures from magazines and coloured paper to make collages. My dad ran an advertising studio and made film posters among other things. In the later part of his life, he realised his dream to be able to make a living from his art. My mum did a lot of handicrafts, and knitted jumpers without any patterns.

A creative person is open to new ideas, new ways of doing things, and can find many different solutions to a problem. Many stages are involved in the creative process, from thinking of new ideas to putting them into practice to refining them.

All ideas that pop into my head I try to write down in my notebook – there have been quite a few books over the years – and I write down briefly what I'm thinking, preferably with a quick sketch to make it clearer. Some of the ideas might not work all the way but you never know when they might come in handy. When I want to put an idea into practice, I start crocheting without giving any thought about what I'd like the end result to be. For me it's important to be able to create patterns and structures without being bound to a specific work. I am more interested in how you can rotate and turn a square to create new repeat patterns. This is the kind of thing that captivates me and what makes me still think that crochet is fantastic! It's fundamentally a simple technique that requires simple tools, such as a crochet hook and some yarn. It's easy to experiment with different stitches and crochet with multiple colours at the same time. Crochet doesn't require a large space and it's easy to take your work with you.

In all the years that I have taught courses, educational programmes and workshops I have seen that many are quick to unravel and start again when they have made a mistake. The mistakes I make can be the start of a new pattern and a new structure. Many of my sample swatches are cases where crocheted 'mistakes' have become something completely new. So all I say is: dare to make mistakes!

I have taken inspiration for my patterns from all kinds of places. It can come to me during a walk in nature or in a city where something catches my attention, such as a shadow play or the façade of a house, and I think about how I could translate it into crochet. Visiting an exhibition or a museum is also something that influences my crochet. Our old textile pattern treasure here in the Nordics appeals to me a lot, where I have found a never-ending source of inspiration.

First published in the United Kingdom
in 2025 by
Batsford
43 Great Ormond Street
London
WC1N 3HZ

An imprint of B. T. Batsford Holdings Limited

Copyright © B. T. Batsford Ltd 2025
Text and images copyright © Maria Gullberg 2025
First published by Bokförlaget Polaris, Denmark 2023
as *Virka rutor!*

English edition published in agreement with Politiken Literary Agency and the Bennet Agency

All rights reserved. No part of this publication may be copied, displayed, extracted, reproduced, utilized, stored in a retrieval system or transmitted in any form or by any means, electronic, mechanical or otherwise including but not limited to photocopying, recording, or scanning without the prior written permission of the publishers.

ISBN 978 1 84994 957 6

A CIP catalogue record for this book is available from the British Library.

10 9 8 7 6 5 4 3 2 1

Reproduction by Rival Colour Ltd, UK
Printed and bound by Toppan Leefung Printing International Ltd, China

This book can be ordered direct from the publisher at www.batsfordbooks.com, or try your local bookshop